D1015029

DUNHAM PUBLIC LIBRARY
WHITESBORO, N.Y.

Dr. Larry Silver's Advice to Parents on

Attention-Deficit Hyperactivity Disorder

Dr. Larry Silver's Advice to Parents on

Attention-Deficit Hyperactivity Disorder

by Larry B. Silver, M.D.
Clinical Professor of Psychiatry and Director of Training
in Child and Adolescent Psychiatry
Georgetown University School of Medicine
Washington, DC

Washington, DC
London, England

Note: The author has worked to ensure that all information in this book concerning drug dosages, schedules, and routes of administration is accurate as of the time of publication and consistent with standards set by the U.S. Food and Drug Administration and the general medical community. As medical research and practice advance, however, therapeutic standards may change. For this reason and because human and mechanical errors sometimes occur, we recommend that readers follow the advice of a physician who is directly involved in their care or the care of a member of their family.

Books published by the American Psychiatric Press, Inc., represent the views and opinions of the individual authors and do not necessarily represent the policies and opinions of the Press or the American Psychiatric Association.

Copyright © 1993 American Psychiatric Press, Inc.
ALL RIGHTS RESERVED
Manufactured in the United States of America on acid-free paper.
97 96 95 92 93 6 5 4 3 2 1

American Psychiatric Press, Inc.
1400 K Street, N.W., Washington, DC 20005

Library of Congress Cataloging-in-Publication Data
Silver, Larry B.
  Dr. Larry Silver's advice to parents on attention-deficit
  hyperactivity disorder / Larry B. Silver.
  p. cm.
  Includes bibliographical references and index.
  ISBN 0-88048-561-2
  1. Attention-deficit hyperactivity disorder—Popular works.
  2. Hyperactive children—Family relationships. I. Title. II. Title:
  Advice to parents on attention-deficit hyperactivity disorder.
  [DNLM: 1. Attention Deficit Disorder with Hyperactivity—
  popular works. WS 350.6 S587d]
    RJ506.H9S55 1993
    18.92'8589—dc20
DNLM/DLC   92-10778
for Library of Congress   CIP

British Library Cataloguing in Publication Data
A CIP record is available from the British Library.

Contents

❖ Adults ❖

❖ Legal Issues ❖

❖ Conclusions ❖

Preface

School is the lifework of children and adolescents. Thus anything that interferes with mastery and success in school will cause stress for the student and his or her family. Attention-deficit hyperactivity disorder (ADHD) can be one of the reasons for academic and school difficulties.

In addition, ADHD can lead to emotional or behavioral problems, difficulty with peer relationships, and difficulty within the family. Unrecognized and untreated, this disorder will interfere greatly with all aspects of the child's or adolescent's life.

Often, by the time a family brings their son or daughter to a health or mental health professional because of academic or school difficulties, there are multiple problems, and each must be identified and addressed. The emotional, social, and family problems may be the most apparent. Parents and/or teachers might report that the child or adolescent cannot sit still or is easily distracted and unable to stay on task. Lack of success in learning academic or study skills may also be found. These problems may be an indirect or direct result of the ADHD or may be secondary to another disorder frequently associated with ADHD, a learning disability.

❖ Case example ❖

John was seven years old and in the first grade when his parents asked me to see him. He was constantly in trouble at school, as well as at home, and he had no friends. John's parents told me that he spent an extra year in preschool and two years in kindergarten because of his "immaturity." When I reviewed the teachers' reports for these four years, I found many references to John's inability to sit still or pay attention; these behaviors were what his teachers described as signs of his immaturity. I also talked with John's first-grade teacher. She described him as restless, saying he was often out of his seat, he never paid attention to her, and he never completed his work. John's mother said that when she did homework with him, she had to remind him to pay attention. He was up and down. She said, "The way I learn is not the way he learns."

John's parents said that he had always been a hyperactive, distractible, and impulsive child. It was his impulsivity that caused John problems at home. He constantly interrupted, he fought with his sister, and he did "wild" things. For example, he would climb out on the roof or climb up on chairs to get things, or he would see something he wanted and dash for it, often bumping into things. From helping him with homework, his parents realized that he could not decode, let alone understand what he read. He held his pencil in an awkward way and still could not form all of his letters. He did not know his number facts nor could he count to 20.

In my sessions with John, he was fidgety and easily distracted by any sound, as well as by the pictures or other objects in my office. It was difficult for him to stay on task when talking or when playing. His choice of play activities and style of interacting with me were appropriate for his age. When I spoke of school, though, he became sad. He felt he was dumb and not as good as the other children in his class. He had had difficulty with easy, early–first-grade reading, writing, and math tasks.

I called John's teacher again. She agreed that his skills were poor, especially for someone already a year older than the other first graders. She insisted that his difficulties were due to his immaturity: "If the parents made him act his age, he would do so much better."

I diagnosed John as having ADHD and prescribed methylphenidate (Ritalin) (medication is discussed in Chapter 13). At a dose of 5 milligrams three times a day, there was a dramatic improvement. John became less active, he was better able to stay on task, and he became more reflective, rather than impulsive. His teacher said the change was remarkable: "He is such a different child." She insisted that the change was due to my psychotherapy and had difficulty accepting the diagnosis, but she admitted that she had never heard of ADHD. John's parents also reported a major change. He was now calm and pleasant at home. He stopped fighting with his sister. He was able to sit and play by himself. He was able to do his homework, and he played much better with the children in the neighborhood.

A full psychological and educational evaluation revealed major learning disabilities that clearly impacted on John's academic ability. His parents learned to be assertive with the school. They had John identified as learning disabled so he would receive the necessary services.

Counseling was started with John's parents. As they better understood their son's problems, they were able to modify their parenting behavior. Brief therapy was started with John. As he better understood his problems and why he was taking medicine and getting special tutoring, he became happier and more pleasant. His behavioral problems at school and at home stopped. He related better to the children his age and began to make friends.

If John's behaviors had been seen only as those of an oppositional child and treated as such, progress would not have been made. Further, such a diagnosis by me would have added support to the school staff's consistent misunderstanding of his behaviors. With the correct diagnoses and interventions (including recognition that John's emotional, social, and family problems were a *result* of ADHD and his learning disabilities and not the *cause* of his problems in school and at home), progress was made.

John's case illustrates the major problems facing parents of a child with ADHD. The diagnosis is often missed. The emotional, social, and family problems are seen as the cause of the behavioral and academic difficulties and not as the consequence of the behavioral and academic difficulties. Often the focus of treatment in school, as well as with mental health professionals, is to treat the behaviors without focusing on the primary causes of the behaviors.

In this book I discuss each of these problems. The primary focus is on ADHD; however, the problems related to possible learning disabilities and the probable secondary emotional, social, and family problems are also stressed.

At present, we are at a clinical "state of the art," rather than "state of the science," when diagnosing and treating ADHD. For this reason, I believe that parents must be as knowledgeable about ADHD and how it is diagnosed and treated as are educational, health, and mental health professionals. Therefore, in this book I review in detail the information that only these professionals usually know. This knowledge will help you work with these professionals and help you best understand your son or daughter. Reading this book may make some parents more knowledgeable about ADHD than a professional they may see. If this happens to you, help to educate him or her. If you are not successful, seek another professional.

To make this book more readable, I have chosen not to write it as a textbook with extensive references. Instead, I have written it as a practical guide that all parents can understand and use. This book is not meant to be a substitute for the more detailed professional guidance and information provided by your family physician or by other health and mental health professionals.

If your child or adolescent also has a learning disability, you might want to read my book for parents called *The Misunderstood Child: A Guide For Parents of Children with Learning Disabilities* (for more information, see Appendix A).

Children and adolescents with ADHD need all of the help they can get. I hope this book helps you to become the supportive and helping parent for your son and daughter that you want to be.

Larry B. Silver, M.D.

Introduction

Chapter 1

Introduction

Many children get up each school morning and promise their parents that they will try to be good in class that day. They do try. But because these children may be hyperactive, distractible, and/or impulsive, their behaviors disrupt class activities, annoy the teacher, and push their classmates away. Such children cannot help their behaviors. Yet, the message they hear is always the same: "Why can't you be good?" *Attention-deficit hyperactivity disorder* or *ADHD* is the current term for this clinical problem. Physicians and other professionals have observed and managed this disorder for many years. However, because its name and our understanding of it have changed over the years, it is useful to start with a historical review.

 ## History ❖

In 1863, Heinrich Hoffman wrote a nursery rhyme about a boy who was restless, fidgety, hyperactive, and a behavioral problem to his family. Today, this boy might be identified as having ADHD.

"Phil, stop acting like a worm,
the table is no place to squirm."
Thus speaks the father to his son,
severely says it, not in fun.
Mother frowns and looks around
although she doesn't make a sound.

But, Philipp will not take advise,
he'll have his way at any price.
He turns,
and churns,
he wiggles
and jiggles
Here and there on the chair;
"Phil, these twists I cannot bear."

Because ADHD is usually associated with school and academic difficulties, the history of this disorder in the United States starts with the study of children and adolescents with learning difficulties. Before 1940, children who had difficulty learning were considered to be either mentally retarded, emotionally disturbed, or socially and culturally disadvantaged. In the early 1940s, however, a fourth possibility was identified: children who had difficulty learning might have a problem with their nervous system.

The initial researchers in this area noted that students in this fourth group had the same learning problems as individuals known to have brain damage, yet they looked normal. It was therefore thought that these children also had brain damage but that the damage was minimal. The term *minimal brain damage* was introduced. Another group of researchers felt that there was little evidence of brain damage. They believed that the problems related to "faulty wiring" within the brain. All of the brain mechanisms were present and operable, but some of the nerve pathways were not functioning the way they should. This concept of faulty functioning (or dysfunction) became the accepted view, and the term *minimal brain dysfunction* or *MBD* was used.

In 1963, a committee was formed to review and present the current understanding of children with MBD. It was sponsored by the National Society for Crippled Children and Adults in cooperation with the Neurological and Sensory Diseases Service Program of the Division of Chronic Diseases of the U.S. Public Health Service. Later, the National Institute of Neurological Diseases and Blindness of the National Institutes of Health joined in this effort. The report on terminology and identification was published in 1966.

In this document, MBD was defined as a disorder of "children of near-average, average, or above-average general intelligence with certain learning or behavioral disabilities ranging from mild to severe, which are associated with deviations of function of the central nervous system. These deviations may manifest themselves by various combinations of impairment in perception, conceptualization, language, memory, and control of attention, impulse, or motor function." Later in this document, the committee discussed emotional and social difficulties associated with this disorder.

Thus, using current concepts, this 1966 document defined MBD as a disorder of children who had

1. Learning disabilities
2. Hyperactivity, distractibility, and impulsivity
3. Emotional and social problems

This overview of the multiple problems that children and adolescents with MBD can have was correct. However, it took another 20 years to understand these problems, during which time researchers from various professions studied these children. Each studied a different part of the problems, and each introduced different terms. Professionals and parents became confused by these many terms.

Learning Problems

Initially, researchers identified primary areas of difficulty in mastering basic academic skills and labeled the students accordingly. If the problems were with reading, the child had *dyslexia*; with writing, *dysgraphia*; and with arithmetic, *dyscalculia*. Later, an effort was made to understand the specific learning difficulties that explained the problems with reading, writing, and arithmetic. Today we refer to the child or adolescent with a presumed neurological basis for their learning difficulties as having a *learning disability*.

Hyperactivity, Distractibility, and Impulsivity

Descriptions of the overactive child date back to the Old Testament. In the United States, the concept was cited in the literature for the first time in 1937 when Bradley, a pediatrician, described children who were recovering from viral encephalitis as becoming hyperactive and/or distractible. The first official acceptance of what is now called ADHD as a clinical diagnostic category was in 1968 with the publication of the *Diagnostic and Statistical Manual of Mental Disorders,* Second Edition (DSM-II), by the American Psychiatric Association. The term *hyperkinetic reaction of childhood (or adolescence)* was used, and with it came the concept of the "hyperactive child." The disorder was characterized by "overactivity, restlessness, distractibility, and short attention span, especially in young children; the behavior usually diminishes in adolescence."

In the Third Edition of this manual (DSM-III), published in 1980, the term for this disorder was changed to *attention deficit disorder* or *ADD* to emphasize that distractibility with a short attention span was the primary clinical issue and that hyperactivity or impulsivity also might be present. Two subtypes of ADD were used: ADD with hyperactivity and ADD without hyperactivity. The definition for ADD with hyperactivity noted that "the child displays, for his or her mental and chronological age, signs of developmentally inappropriate inattention, impulsivity, and hyperactivity."

Establishing a diagnosis of ADD required that the onset of the behaviors occurred before the age of seven and that the behaviors had been present for at least six months. DSM-III listed behaviors characteristic of each component: inattention, impulsivity, and hyperactivity. To be diagnosed as having this disorder, a child had to show evidence of at least one of these three behaviors.

The revision of the Third Edition (DSM-III-R) was published in 1987. In it the term was changed to *attention-deficit hyperactivity disorder* to reflect that, although distractibility is the primary issue, hyperactivity is also an important factor of the disorder. The diagnosis still requires the onset of behaviors before age seven, but the child or adolescent must show at least eight of a list of 14 behaviors for at least six months. These behaviors are discussed in detail in Chapter 3.

The committee preparing the Fourth Edition (DSM-IV), scheduled to be published in 1994, is considering several issues. Research data suggest that children with only distractibility have a different outcome than those who also have hyperactivity and/or impulsivity. Thus there might be two different diagnostic categories used to reflect the different outcomes. It is hoped that, as brain research adds new understanding to the concept of ADHD specifically and to the broader concept of attentional disorders, this diagnostic category will be further clarified.

Emotional, Social, and Family Problems

Children and adolescents with ADHD plus possibly a learning disability will become frustrated in school. They might eventually develop emotional or behavioral problems, as well as peer and other social problems. Their family members will become frustrated as well. Their parents might disagree on the best way to raise or to discipline them. Eventually, the surface problems are the only ones seen, and the school and academic problems are considered to be a result of the emotional and family problems. In reality, the emotional, social, and family problems are not *causing* the school and academic difficulties, they are a *consequence* of the school and academic difficulties with the resulting experiences of frustration and failure. It is this differentiation between cause and symptom that must be stressed with children and adolescents who have ADHD.

❖ **The Total Child**

Returning to the descriptions and perspectives noted in the 1966 monograph on MBD, we know these children and adolescents have a group of problems often found together. The common theme for most is that they have a learning disability. In addition, some will have ADHD, and most will develop secondary emotional, social, and family problems.

- Learning Disabilities
- ADHD
- Secondary Emotional, Social, and Family Problems

We also now know more about the frequency with which these difficulties occur. Of all children and adolescents with learning disabilities, it is estimated that between 20% and 25% will also have ADHD.

On the other hand, of all the children and adolescents with ADHD, it is estimated that between 50% and 80% will also have a learning disability. In other words,

- If a child or adolescent has a learning disability, there is a 20% to 25% chance that he or she will also have ADHD.
- If a child or adolescent has ADHD, there is a 50% to 80% chance that he or she will also have a learning disability.

Thus when a health or mental health professional establishes the diagnosis of ADHD, it is critical that he or she explore whether the student also has a learning disability. From a preventive-medicine view, *the clinician must rule out a learning disability with each individual diagnosed as having ADHD.*

Children and adolescents with ADHD often develop emotional, social, and family problems. If they also have a learning disability, the probability of developing such problems is even greater.

❖ **Other Related Disorders** ❖

A small percentage of children and adolescents with ADHD may also have a chronic tic disorder called *Tourette syndrome.* However, about 50% of individuals with Tourette syndrome also have ADHD. This syndrome is characterized by frequently changing motor (muscular) and vocal tics. The onset is usually before the age of 21 years, and the individual has recurrent, involuntary, rapid, purposeless motor movements affecting multiple muscle groups. In addition, he or she might have one or more vocal tics. There is a variation in the intensity of the symptoms over weeks to months (called *waxing and waning*). Establishing the diagnosis requires that the tics have lasted for more than one year. Usually, there is a family history of the problem.

Some children and adolescents with ADHD may have a seizure disorder. Several types of seizures are possible. *Grand mal* seizures (generally called *epilepsy*) are characterized by major convulsions, with intermittent spasms of all body muscles, followed by a jerking motion of these muscles. After the seizure, the child is asleep or lethargic. When the child wakes up, he or she is confused and disoriented and has no memory of the event. During a grand mal seizure, some people lose bladder or bowel control. Many report a brief sensory experience, or "aura," before the seizure.

Petit mal seizures are brief attacks, with momentary loss of consciousness, often associated with symmetrical jerking movements of the eyelids or some other part of the body. Sometimes no muscle activity occurs, just the brief loss of consciousness, and the child will probably not fall over or fall down. Once the episode ends, the child is alert and has no memory loss except for the short span of the seizure.

Psychomotor seizures are accompanied by attacks of a wide variety of confusing behaviors. Explosive, aggressive actions may occur. The child is confused and disoriented after the episode. Or a child might have a *focal* seizure, which is characterized by convulsions confined to a single limb or muscle group, or to a specific type of sensory disturbance. Finally, a child may have what are called *partial* seizures. These seizures are very focused in the brain and can cause brief changes in sensation, perception, thinking, speech, memory, affect, motor activity, and/or behavior. If the child also loses consciousness, these are called *complex partial* seizures.

Still others with ADHD might show evidence of an *obsessive-compulsive disorder*. This problem is characterized by persistent obsessive or compulsive behaviors. *Obsessions* are characterized by recurrent and persistent ideas, thoughts, impulses, or images that are experienced as intrusive and senseless behaviors. The child may attempt to ignore or suppress such thoughts or impulses and recognizes that the obsessions are the product of his or her own mind. *Compulsions* are repetitive, purposeful, and intentional behaviors that are performed in response to an obsession, according to certain rules, or in a stereotyped fashion. The behavior is designed to neutralize or to prevent discomfort or some dreaded event or situation. In addition, the child recognizes that his or her behavior is excessive or unreasonable.

❖   **Prevalence of ADHD**   ❖

Because of the changing criteria for establishing the diagnosis of ADHD and the absence of a reliable or valid diagnostic method, no clear data are available on its prevalence. When similar rating scales are used and teachers are used as the raters, the prevalence of ADHD in the school-age population appears to range from 10% to 20%. If parents are the source of the information, the prevalence rates appear to be higher, perhaps as high as 30%.

Studies have shown that ADHD is more common among boys. In clinic-referred samples of patients, the ratio of boys to girls with ADHD has been reported to be from 2:1 to 10:1. However, among nonreferred children (in community surveys), studies have shown the ratio to be closer to 3:1. This higher rate of boys among clinic samples as compared with community surveys probably reflects referral bias. Boys are more likely than girls to be aggressive and antisocial, and such behavior is more likely to lead to a referral.

It may also be that these data reflect the underidentification of ADHD in girls. The clinical characteristics of girls with ADHD show that, despite attentional problems similar to those of boys with ADHD, they are less intrusive, exhibit fewer aggressive symptoms, and, thus, are less likely to come to the attention of their teachers or other professionals. It is possible that the group of students most often not recognized, referred, or diagnosed are girls who are only distractible.

❖ Life History of ADHD ❖

The longitudinal data are less complete for all of the reasons discussed above. In addition, the concept of ADHD in adults is relatively new and, thus, has not been followed until recently. Current data suggest that about 50% of children with ADHD show a decrease or loss of the behaviors at puberty. The reason for this improvement is not known. Still, 50% of these children will continue to have ADHD as adolescents. Further, it appears that between 30% and 70% of these adolescents will continue to have these behaviors into adulthood.

❖ Summary ❖

The possibility that a child or adolescent with ADHD might have a learning disability is so high that this disability must be ruled out whenever the diagnosis of ADHD is made.

Introduction

ADHD and learning disabilities are related disorders, but they are not the same disorders. A learning disability impacts on the basic psychological processes needed to learn. ADHD results in behaviors that can make the individual unavailable for learning experiences or for successful functioning in the classroom. The treatment for one of these problems will not treat the other. The medications that treat ADHD will not correct the learning disability. The special education approaches used to treat the learning disabilities will not improve the ADHD. Some professionals and parents still use these terms interchangeably. This should not be done.

ADHD is a *life disability*. Hyperactivity, distractibility, and/or impulsivity are not just school problems; they are life problems. These behaviors interfere with classroom learning and behavior, but they also interfere with family life, peer interactions, and all other activities in the child's life. This concept is important when we consider treatment. If the clinician treats the ADHD during school hours and months only, the individual might do well in school but continue to have a behavioral problem at home and with friends.

For some, ADHD might be a *lifetime disability*. We now know that about 50% of children with ADHD will continue to have this disorder as adolescents. Only about half appear to improve with the brain maturational spurt at puberty. Of these adolescents, it is estimated that between 30% and 70% will continue to have ADHD as an adult. This concept of adult or residual ADHD is established. We once had the belief (or wish) that these children outgrew their problems at puberty. We now know that this is not true for all.

ADHD is a complex problem. It is critical that any professional working with your son or daughter be aware of this total child or adolescent in his or her total world when treatment is provided. It is equally critical that any related disorder—learning disabilities or secondary emotional, social, and family problems—be recognized and treated as well.

It is of equal importance that you, as parents, understand your total son or daughter in his or her total world. If the education, health, or mental health professional is only focusing on one part of your child or adolescent, you must be informed enough to stress that the other problem areas must also be understood and helped.

11

Diagnosis

Chapter 2

Difficulties That Would Suggest ADHD

A s discussed in Chapter 1, the official DSM-III-R diagnostic guidelines describe the essential features of attention-deficit hyperactivity disorder (ADHD) as "developmentally inappropriate degrees of inattention, impulsiveness, and hyperactivity. People with the disorder generally display some disturbances in each of these areas, but to varying degrees." It is important to understand that some children and adolescents will have one, some two, and some all three of these behaviors. *It is not necessary to have all three behaviors.* A child can be relaxed, even hypoactive, and have ADHD if he or she is distractible and/or impulsive. Perhaps the ADHD individual most often missed is the child or adolescent who is only distractible, with no evidence of hyperactivity or impulsivity.

❖ What Are These Behaviors? ❖

Hyperactivity

We used to describe hyperactive children as those who ran around and could not stand or sit still. Physicians were taught, "If you went out to your waiting room and it was in shambles, you knew you had a hyperactive child." We now know that most children with ADHD are not that obviously active. They are more likely to be fidgety. If you look, you will see that some part of their body is always in motion, often purposeless motion. Their fingers are tapping, or they are playing with their pencil. While they are sitting, their legs are swinging, or they are twisting or squirming in their chair. Teachers may report that they sit with one knee on the floor. You may notice that your child has never sat still through a whole meal in his or her entire life. Some appear to be verbally hyperactive, talking constantly.

Distractibility

Children and adolescents with ADHD have difficulty knowing what to attend to in their environment and what to block out. All stimuli come into their brains and compete to be focused on. Therefore, they are distractible; they have difficulty sustaining attention (thus a short attention span) and difficulty staying on task.

A child or adolescent with ADHD may be auditorily distractible and/or visually distractible. If auditorily distractible, he or she will hear and respond to sounds that most of us would hear and tune out. Teachers report that if someone in the back of the classroom is tapping a pencil or talking, others can ignore it but this child must turn and listen. If someone is talking in the hall or someone is dribbling a basketball outside on the playground, somehow this student looks up and asks, "What's that?" You may find that when you are reading a story to your child or when he or she is doing homework, every sound is responded to—a floorboard creaking in another room or a car horn a block away.

If the child or adolescent is visually distractible, he or she might be distracted by the design on a rug or a picture or other objects in the room. If outside, he or she will notice birds flying, clouds going by, or the trees and will not stay focused on the appropriate activity. You might observe that when you send this child to get something, somehow on the way he or she sees something and starts to play with it. Then the child sees something else and goes to it. He or she never gets to the original destination.

Some children who are distractible appear to be able to attend to certain tasks for long periods of time. Parents might question whether their son or daughter is truly distractible when he or she can spend hours watching television or playing a video game. However, such tasks are usually ones the child enjoys and for which the motivation is high. It appears that to be able to attend like this, such children have to apply extra "filters" to block out the sounds they do not want to attend to. They appear to be in a trance. For example, you can talk to your son, but he does not respond. You find that you have to shake him or stand between him and the activity to get his attention. Then he may say "Huh?" and respond.

Some adolescents with distractibility insist that they can study best with music playing in the background. Parents question how they could be distractible if they can work with such noise. However, so many adolescents have used the same reason to explain why they do this that I now believe that their explanation may be correct. They say that if the room is very quiet they hear every little noise or voice. If they play music in the background, it blocks out these sounds and all they hear is the steady sound of the music. They believe that they are less distracted and better able to work.

Parents may report that their child experiences what I call "sensory overload." Noisy environments (like birthday parties, shopping malls, the circus, or sports events) can cause such children to get upset and irritable. They might cover their ears or want to leave, or they might complain of a headache. It appears that if there is too much auditory stimulation they cannot block out these inputs, and they feel over-loaded. Adolescents and young adults may describe the same experience at a party or in a bar. The music playing and people talking cause an overload, and they feel uncomfortable or anxious.

Impulsivity

Children and adolescents with impulsivity appear not to be able to reflect before they talk or act. Thus they do not learn from experience because they cannot delay their action long enough to recall past experiences and consequences. They say something and may be sorry they said it before they are finished. They get upset and act by hitting or throwing something. They turn quickly and knock things over. They may fail to wait their turn and speak out or may answer a question before the teacher finishes asking the question. Because of the impulsive behavior, they appear to have poor judgment and may be accident prone. Parents have even been accused of child abuse because of the frequent injuries their child gets because of these impulsive behaviors.

There are several clinical problems that may be seen with children and adolescents who are impulsive, including bed-wetting, fire-setting and fascination with and/or playing with fire, and stealing. They also might lie more than is appropriate for their age or hide or hoard food in their room. There is no clear explanation for the association of these behaviors with impulsivity; however, they are often found with children and adolescents who are impulsive.

❖ **How Is Information** ❖
on Behavior Obtained?

It is difficult for clinicians to observe hyperactivity, distractibility, or impulsivity in their office. In the office of a general physician or pediatrician, the child probably will be seen for five to seven minutes. He or she may have learned to be very alert in this office or run the risk of being stuck, gaged, or poked. Thus the child may be quiet and attentive. If the office is that of a general psychiatrist, child and adolescent psychiatrist, or other mental health professional, the room is likely to be quiet with a one-to-one interaction with an adult. It is important to understand that if hyperactivity, distractibility, and/or impulsivity are not seen in the clinician's office, this professional should not conclude that they do not exist.

The best source of observational data is from real-life situations. Professionals must learn from parents, teachers, tutors, and other adults who interact with the child or adolescent and who can describe what he or she is like in structured and unstructured situations. Each can describe the child's behaviors at school, in the home, and with friends. The clinician should ask you, the parents, to describe what you live with. If realistic, a visit by the clinician to the school to observe is helpful. If this is not possible, she or he should talk to the teacher or ask the parents to get the information from the teachers. There are rating scales and other informational forms that clinicians might give parents or teachers to complete. Such data can help in the diagnostic process. These instruments are discussed in Chapter 3.

❖ All That Looks Like ADHD ❖
Is Not ADHD

There are many reasons why children and adolescents might be hyperactive, distractible, and/or impulsive. It is important to understand that not all individuals who show these behaviors have ADHD. Each of the related disorders discussed in Chapter 1 can also cause these behaviors. This concept will be introduced here and expanded on in detail in Chapter 3.

Learning Disabilities

As mentioned in Chapter 1, there is a high probability that children or adolescents with ADHD will also have learning disabilities. The behaviors caused by the learning disabilities could look like ADHD. For example, DSM-III-R lists the following characteristics for ADHD, but each could also be a reflection of a learning disability:

- Not finishing class work
- Having difficulty organizing work
- Appearing to be not listening
- Doing messy work

In the next chapter, this process of sorting out the different possibilities in order to establish the correct diagnosis is expanded to include specific types of learning disabilities that could appear to be ADHD.

Emotional Problems

Anxiety or depression can be expressed by behaviors of increased muscle activity, inattentiveness or distractibility, or irritability and impulsivity. In addition, children and adolescents with behavioral problems such as oppositional defiant disorder or conduct disorder may appear to have ADHD or may indeed have ADHD as well (this is discussed in more detail in Chapter 3). It is important, therefore, to decide if the observed behaviors are a result of a primary emotional or behavioral problem, the result of an emotional or behavioral problem that develops because of ADHD (plus possible learning disabilities), or the result of ADHD.

❖   # Summary   ❖

It is possible that too many children and adolescents are diagnosed as having ADHD. The reason this happens might be that some clinicians diagnose hyperactive, distractible, and/or impulsive children as having ADHD without exploring other possible causes for their behaviors. The teacher tells the parent that the child cannot sit still or stay on task. The parent reports this to the family doctor who recommends medication to treat the ADHD. No effort is made to think through what else might be causing these behaviors.

It is equally possible that too many children and adolescents who are hyperactive, distractible, and/or impulsive are not diagnosed properly as having ADHD because clinicians see the presenting emotional, social, and/or family problems and establish a psychiatric diagnosis without considering whether these problems might be caused by ADHD plus possible learning disabilities.

It is as important to diagnose correctly an individual with ADHD as it is not to diagnose incorrectly an individual with ADHD. In Chapter 3, I discuss this diagnostic process.

Chapter 3

How Is the Diagnosis
of ADHD Established?

Presently, there are no formal tests to establish the diagnosis of attention-deficit hyperactivity disorder (ADHD). There are no specific physical findings; no blood, urine, brain imaging, or brain wave studies (electroencephalograms); and no neurological findings that establish the diagnosis. There are excellent rating scales that can identify whether the child or adolescent is hyperactive, distractible, and/or impulsive; however, these rating scales may not differentiate between ADHD and other possible causes for these behaviors. The best diagnostic technique is the clinical history. This clinical history must include observational data from the school and the family.

As discussed in Chapter 2, there are many possible causes of hyperactivity, distractibility, and/or impulsivity in children and adolescents. Moreover, many individuals with ADHD also have a learning disability, and certain types of learning disabilities can result in hyperactive or distractible behaviors. The evaluation process must include a consideration of all of the possible causes of the observed and reported hyperactivity, distractibility, and/or impulsivity.

In order for you to work closely with the professional evaluating your son or daughter for ADHD, I must go into detail on the other possible causes of these behaviors and the approach that should be used in establishing the diagnosis. You must be knowledgeable to help your clinician help your daughter or son.

❖ "Official" Criteria for ADHD ❖

The official guidelines used by professionals to diagnose ADHD are from the official classification system, the *Diagnostic and Statistical Manual of Mental Disorders*. As discussed in Chapter 1, the current edition of this manual is a revision of the Third Edition, and so you will hear of "DSM-III-R." Don't let the title of the manual upset you. ADHD is identified as a psychiatric disorder and, thus, listed in this manual. According to these guidelines, to be diagnosed as having ADHD, your son or daughter must meet the three criteria described in Table 1.

I believe there are difficulties with the DSM-III-R criteria. First, each of the listed behaviors could be caused by an emotional problem, a learning disability, and/or environmental influences. Second, recent research suggests that ADHD may be but one aspect of a group of "attentional disorders." Thus a broader clinical concept may be needed. However, for now, DSM-III-R is the official diagnostic manual, and the criteria listed must be used by health and mental health professionals.

As much as I do not like to admit it, there are pediatricians and other family physicians who do not fully understand ADHD. It becomes critical that you understand what it is and what it is not so that you can work with (perhaps, at times help) your physician in the evaluation process. Therefore, I will go into more medical detail than might be considered by some as necessary for parents.

❖ The Differential Diagnostic Process ❖

The three presenting behaviors of ADHD are hyperactivity, distractibility, and impulsivity. Let's look again at each of these behaviors before focusing on their possible causes.

Hyperactivity

Most hyperactive children and adolescents are not running around the room or jumping on the furniture. They appear to be fidgety. Their fingers are tapping; their pencil is moving; their leg is swinging; they are up and down from their desk or the dinner table. Something is al-

Table 1. DSM-III-R diagnostic criteria for attention-deficit hyperactivity disorder

A. A disturbance of at least six months during which at least eight of the following are present:

1. Often fidgets with hands or feet or squirms in seat (in adolescents, may be limited to subjective feelings of restlessness)
2. Has difficulty remaining seated when required to do so
3. Is easily distracted by extraneous stimuli
4. Has difficulty awaiting turn in games or group situations
5. Often blurts out answers to questions before they have been completed
6. Has difficulty following through on instructions from others (not due to oppositional behavior or failure of comprehension), e.g., fails to finish chores
7. Has difficulty sustaining attention in tasks or play activities
8. Often shifts from one uncompleted activity to another
9. Has difficulty playing quietly
10. Often talks excessively
11. Often interrupts or intrudes on others, e.g., butts into other children's games
12. Often does not seem to listen to what is being said to him or her
13. Often loses things necessary for tasks or activities at school or at home, e.g., toys, pencils, books, assignments
14. Often engages in physically dangerous activities without considering possible consequences (not for the purpose of thrill-seeking), e.g., runs into street without looking

B. Onset before the age of seven.

C. Does not meet the criteria for a pervasive developmental disorder [a more serious psychiatric disorder].

Source. Adapted from American Psychiatric Association: *Diagnostic and Statistical Manual of Mental Disorders,* Third Edition, Revised. Washington, DC, American Psychiatric Association, 1987, pp. 52–53. Used with permission.

ways in motion. Parents may report that these children are equally restless at night, moving about the bed. With adolescents, the fidgety behaviors may be less apparent; however, they are there. An anxious child can be hyperactive; not all fidgety students have ADHD.

Distractibility

There are many reasons why a child or adolescent might be distractible; ADHD is only one of them. It is important, therefore, to look at these other reasons for distractibility. In Chapter 8, I discuss the broader concept of "attentional disorders." For now, let's look at two general groups: internal distractibility and external distractibility.

- **Internal distractibility**
  - Daydreaming
  - Auditory perception disability
  - Cognitive disinhibition (I'll explain this term later.)
- **External distractibility**
  - Environmental overload
  - ADHD

Internal distractibility.   Daydreaming is not uncommon with children and adolescents. Many students escape into their thoughts and then realize that they have not heard a word the teacher was saying. The teacher might comment that such a student is not paying attention. In reality, though, the daydreaming might reflect family or other stress, an emotional disorder, or the excitement of an event (such as the day before a holiday or vacation).

Auditory perception disabilities are discussed in detail in Chapter 4. Children with such disabilities may have an auditory figure-ground problem: that is, if there is more than one sound in the environment (students talking, activity in the hall, teacher talking), they may have difficulty knowing which sounds to listen to. The teacher might be into his or her third sentence before students with this disorder realize the teacher is talking and attend. By then, they are lost and are described as not paying attention. Another auditory perception disability is an auditory lag. Individuals with this disability need to concentrate on what they hear for an instant longer than others do before they understand it. Thus at any given time they are concentrating on what they just heard while trying to hold on to what is coming in next. They cannot keep up this process and eventually miss parts of what is said. For example, the teacher reviews a lesson plan. As soon as the teacher is finished, these students might need to ask questions about something the teacher just explained and are accused of not paying attention.

Some individuals have difficulty inhibiting their internal thought processes. (There is no established term for this difficulty; I call it *cognitive disinhibition.*) Their internal thoughts protrude into their conscious behaviors. They are in class and suddenly start to talk about something that appears to be off the topic. Younger children might suddenly start to talk about dinosaurs or space, or they might begin to laugh or become paranoid because of their internal thoughts. This disorder is most often found among individuals with a more serious psychiatric disorder called *pervasive developmental disorder.* Before pervasive developmental disorder is identified, the child might be described as someone who is distractible and who never stays on task.

External distractibility. The best example of an environmental overload occurred when many educational systems decided that the "open classroom" would create a more stimulating environment for learning. For many students without other behaviors characteristic of ADHD, the noise and multiple auditory inputs created distractibility. They could not pay attention to their teacher or to their work. The stimulation of the many work stations both in their classroom and in adjacent spaces often became visually overstimulating and caused distractibility. These students did not have ADHD, but they appeared to be distractible.

For some students, sitting next to an open window or a door that is open to the hall can be distracting. For other students, a classroom that the teacher cannot control (one that is noisy or has students moving around) can be too much of a sensory overload to permit attending to task. The same situation might exist for students who like to do their homework in the family room with the television playing and siblings running around or talking.

Impulsivity

Impulsivity is described as the inability (or difficulty with being able) to stop and reflect before speaking or acting. Thus the impulsive child or adolescent interrupts the teacher or parent, answers a question with the first thought that occurs, or says something and then is immediately sorry he or she said it. This individual might get frustrated or angry and yell, throw something, or hit someone. He or she never learns from experience, because to learn from experience one has to stop and think about past experiences and consequences before speaking or acting. The impulsive child or adolescent does not have the luxury of the time to think first.

Impulsivity is characteristic of many psychiatric disorders and can reflect immaturity, anxiety, depression, or learned (and possibly rewarded) behavior. This behavior might reflect an immature or dysfunctional nervous system. One such dysfunction is ADHD.

❖   **Differential Diagnosis**   ❖

Emotional Issues

Anxiety. The most common cause of hyperactivity, distractibility, or impulsivity with children, adolescents, and adults is anxiety. Anxiety can be a reflection of psychological stress or conflict or reflective of a specific psychiatric disorder. If hyperactivity, distractibility, and impulsivity are a reflection of anxiety, the diagnosis is not ADHD. When people are anxious, they can be restless and motorically active. For children, motor activity might be the primary way of reflecting anxiety. In addition, it is difficult for people to pay attention when they feel anxious. They might daydream or try to watch television or read a book. However, it is difficult to stay on the task or to pay attention to what is heard, seen, or read. Anxiety can also cause people to be irritable and appear to be impulsive.

Depression. The next most common cause of hyperactivity, distractibility, or impulsivity with children, adolescents, or adults is depression. Depression might reflect a psychological conflict or stress or might reflect a specific psychiatric disorder. Again, if hyperactivity, distractibility, and impulsivity are a reflection of a depressive process, the diagnosis is not ADHD. Depression can be expressed at all ages and may be reflected in an agitated or in a withdrawn form (called *psychomotor retardation*). If agitated, the individual may be restless and active. He or she will have difficulty concentrating or staying on task. Some may be irritable and act impulsively. If in the withdrawn phase of depression, the individual might feel so involved with his or her feelings and/or thoughts that he or she has difficulty paying attention to what is going on or with communicating with people.

Sometimes it is difficult to separate out depression from ADHD. The case of "Chris" is a good example of this:

❖ Case example ❖

Chris was ten years old and in the fifth grade when his parents asked me to see him. He had been in individual and group therapy for two years because of emotional problems. Chris was unhappy in school, and he wasn't doing his school work in class or at home. A psychological and educational evaluation done by his school system 18 months earlier showed evidence of visual perception, visual motor, and fine motor difficulties, but the evaluation team concluded that "his weaknesses were not great enough nor his skill levels behind enough to qualify for services."

From speaking with his parents and reviewing his school records, I learned that Chris had been labeled as hyperactive and distractible in preschool and kindergarten. His first-grade teacher described him as overactive and unable to stay on task. His second-grade teacher said much the same thing. Third grade was described as a terrible year for Chris; he got into fights, disrupted the classroom, and did not complete his work. Fourth grade was no better. Chris was falling further behind in school skills and strategies. His teachers blamed this on his behavior and his "refusal" to sit still or pay attention.

Chris was adopted by his family at age four. At age three, he had been taken from his mother and placed in a foster home because her boyfriend had sexually abused him. His mother had also been neglectful, often leaving him alone. The social agency reports indicated that his mother had used alcohol and drugs during this pregnancy.

Chris's adoptive parents placed him in therapy to help him cope with his past. The school professionals believed that all of his academic and behavioral problems were secondary to his emotional problems.

During my psychiatric assessment sessions with Chris, he spoke openly of his past. He knew about it and felt that he no longer worried about it: "I talked it all over in my therapy. It is behind me and this is my family now and forever. I like them." I could find no evidence of emotional conflicts related to his past. He did, however, speak of frustrations in school. He didn't like school; he felt he wasn't as smart as the other kids. He was aware that he had problems sitting still in class and that any noise or activity could easily distract him. He blamed the fighting on the other kids teasing him.

Because Chris seemed to have had a chronic and pervasive history of hyperactivity and distractibility, the diagnosis *could* be ADHD. His mother's alcohol and substance abuse during pregnancy might have caused a neurological problem manifested by ADHD and learning disabilities. However, other factors suggested that Chris was still dealing with what is called a *posttraumatic stress disorder* related to his early childhood; the hyperactivity and distractibility might be a reflection of his anxiety and/or depression.

After discussing these issues with his therapist, I spoke with Chris and his parents in a family session. We agreed to a trial on medication to help clarify the issues (medication is discussed in Chapter 13). I prescribed 5 milligrams of methylphenidate (Ritalin) to be taken three times a day. From the first dose, Chris became calmer, less distractible, and better able to stay on task. His parents and all of his teachers noticed the significant improvement.

After I made several contacts with his school system, Chris was identified as having a learning disability and was placed in a special education program. With this change and the use of the medication, the fighting and other behavioral problems at school stopped.

Behavioral Issues

It is estimated that about 50% of children who meet the DSM-III-R criteria for ADHD will also meet the DSM-III-R criteria for oppositional defiant disorder or conduct disorder. Similarly, most children who meet the criteria for these disruptive behavioral disorders will meet the criteria for ADHD. The critical question for the mental health professional is whether these are separate disorders that coexist in the same child (called *comorbidity*) or whether they represent different clinical pictures of the same underlying difficulty.

The issue is confused further by the fact that children and adolescents with ADHD are initially brought to the attention of different types of health professionals depending on whether they also have disruptive behavioral problems. The parents of a child with ADHD but without such disruptive behaviors will most likely first discuss their son's or daughter's problems with their family physician. On the other hand, the parents of a child with ADHD plus a disruptive behavioral problem will most likely be referred to a mental health professional by someone in the school. Therefore, if the definition of ADHD is established by mental health clinicians and based on the children they see, it is likely that the most obvious behaviors—the disruptive behaviors—will be focused on. This, in turn, will result in a self-fulfilling prophecy that further encourages educators to identify ADHD on the basis of these disruptive behavioral problems.

Recent research supports the belief that ADHD should be identified as separate from oppositional defiant disorder or conduct disorder. Evidence shows that children can have any of these disorders alone but that they are more likely to occur in combination with each other. Each must be clarified and the treatment plan must address each disorder. To focus on the other disorders and not treat the ADHD will not be successful. Because you will hear of these two disorders and, possibly, your son or daughter will be labeled as having one of them, I need to go into more detail on each. Again, I use the guidelines in DSM-III-R because these are the ones that professionals use.

Oppositional defiant disorder. The essential feature of oppositional defiant disorder is a recurring pattern of negativistic, hostile, and defiant behavior that has become developmentally stable for at least six months. These symptoms must be present to a degree that is excessive or deviant for the child's mental age. The DSM-III-R diagnostic criteria for an oppositional defiant disorder are presented in Table 2.

Conduct disorder. It is not uncommon for a child to be diagnosed as having ADHD in early childhood, oppositional defiant disorder in later childhood, and finally conduct disorder in late childhood or early adolescence. The essential feature of conduct disorder is a persistent pattern of conduct in which the basic rights of others and major age-appropriate societal norms or rules are violated. It is usually pervasive, occurring in school, the community, with peers, and at home. Physical

---

Table 2.   DSM-III-R diagnostic criteria for oppositional defiant disorder

---

A. A disturbance of at least six months during which at least five of the following are present:

1. Often loses temper

2. Often argues with adults

3. Often actively defies or refuses adult requests or rules, e.g., refuses to do chores at home

4. Often deliberately does things that annoy other people, e.g., grabs other children's hats

5. Often blames others for his or her own mistakes

6. Is often touchy or easily annoyed by others

7. Is often angry and resentful

8. Is often spiteful or vindictive

9. Often swears or uses obscene language

B. Does not meet the criteria for conduct disorder and does not occur exclusively during the course of a psychotic disorder or significant depression.

Source. Adapted from American Psychiatric Association: *Diagnostic and Statistical Manual of Mental Disorders,* Third Edition, Revised. Washington, DC, American Psychiatric Association, 1987, pp. 57–58. Used with permission.

aggression and physical destructiveness are more common in this disorder than they are in oppositional defiant disorder. The DSM-III-R criteria for conduct disorder are presented in Table 3.

Table 3. DSM-III-R diagnostic criteria for conduct disorder

A. A disturbance of conduct lasting at least six months, during which at least three of the following have been present:

1. Has stolen without confrontation of a victim on more than one occasion (including forgery)

2. Has run away from home overnight at least twice while living in parental or parental surrogate home (or once without returning)

3. Often lies (other than to avoid physical or sexual abuse)

4. Has deliberately engaged in fire-setting

5. Is often truant from school (for older person, absent from work)

6. Has broken into someone else's house, building, or car

7. Has deliberately destroyed others' property (other than by fire-setting)

8. Has been physically cruel to animals

9. Has forced someone into sexual activity with him or her

10. Has used a weapon in more than one fight

11. Often initiates physical fights

12. Has stolen with confrontation of a victim, e.g., mugging, purse-snatching, extortion, armed robbery

13. Has been physically cruel to people

B. If 18 or older, does not meet criteria for antisocial personality disorder.

Source. Adapted from American Psychiatric Association: *Diagnostic and Statistical Manual of Mental Disorders,* Third Edition, Revised. Washington, DC, American Psychiatric Association, 1987, p. 55. Used with permission.

❖ **Neurological Factors** ❖
Other Than ADHD

Learning Disability

One type of learning disability—auditory perception disability—was discussed earlier in this chapter. A child or adolescent with this disability can be seen as distractible. Other types of learning disabilities might make it difficult for the student to understand, organize school work, or complete assignments. The student might appear not to be staying on task when the real issue is that he or she is on task but cannot do the work. If the student with a learning disability does not understand the work and cannot do the work, he or she may become anxious. This anxiety can cause hyperactive or distractible behavior. In this case, it is the anxiety caused by the learning disability that is causing the behaviors and not ADHD.

Sometimes after the diagnosis of ADHD is correctly established and the student is started on the appropriate medication, the hyperactivity and/or distractibility decrease; however, the associated learning disability may not have been diagnosed. Suddenly, the student can sit in class and attend to his or her work, but he or she does not understand the work and cannot do it. He or she becomes anxious and starts to fidget or to daydream. The teacher might believe that the medication is no longer working. It is important to understand that even children or adolescents with ADHD and on the proper medication can become anxious or depressed.

Sensory Integrative Disorder

Some individuals with ADHD and/or learning disabilities also have what is called a *sensory integrative disorder*. This disorder is discussed in more detail in Chapter 4; however, I need to give you some information here to explain why this disorder must be considered when a child or adolescent is seen as hyperactive.

Individuals with ADHD plus sensory integrative disorder have difficulty receiving and processing perceptions that are needed to orient and move their body in space and to use their muscles for complex tasks. The three perceptions impacted on with this disorder are those needed for receiving and understanding touch (tactile perception), for receiving and understanding information from the muscles and joints (proprioception perception), and for receiving and understanding information on the position of one's head in space and one's body in gravity (vestibular perception). These individuals may be tactilely sensitive or defensive; they might have difficulty moving their body appropriately in space; they might have difficulty doing tasks that require muscle planning, such as buttoning or tying; or they might have difficulty orienting their body to their head position. If tactilely sensitive or defensive they will be overly aware of tags on their clothes, a belt, or the texture of their clothes; thus they may wiggle or move about, appearing to be hyperactive. They might be unsure of their body and its position in space; thus they might move about, trying to become more comfortable. Therefore, children with sensory integrative disorder might be fidgety. In these situations, the hyperactivity and fidgety behaviors are a reflection of this disorder and not of ADHD.

❖ Rating Scales as Part ❖ of the Diagnostic Process

Rating scales are popular when assessing children's behaviors. In addition to the clinical interview, these behavioral rating scales provide information from people who know the child well, such as parents and teachers. They are seen as efficient, and they are based on established norms.

The question is, what is being measured or assessed? The data from a rating scale might show the individual to be hyperactive, distractible, and/or impulsive, but the clinician still does not know why these behaviors are present. Thus if rating scales are used in the diagnostic process, they must be considered only as a source of observational data, not as the diagnostic process itself.

There are advantages to using rating scales in clinical practice. First, there are normative data that permit the clinician to determine the degree of deviance of a particular child within the population of same-age and same-sex children. This is essential to the diagnosis of ADHD because many ADHD characteristics occur to some degree in children without the disorder. Second, rating scales can be a convenient means for collapsing information about a child across situations and time intervals into units of information of value to diagnosis. It would be difficult to collect direct observations of children over diverse settings and over several months for clinical purposes. Finally, rating scales provide a convenient means for evaluating a person's responses to clinical interventions.

Because rating scales are often used by clinicians, let me review briefly the more popular ones. If you are asked to fill out such a rating scale, be sure to question what it measures. You may need to remind the clinician that the information obtained might clarify that your son or daughter is hyperactive, distractible, and/or impulsive, but the information will not establish the diagnosis of ADHD.

Parent Rating Scales

The Conners series of parent rating scales are the most widely used. There are three forms: the original 93-item version, the revised 48-item version, and the ten-item Abbreviated Symptom Questionnaire. It should be kept in mind that these scales were developed when an earlier edition of DSM (the diagnostic manual) was in use and the focus is primarily on hyperactivity.

The Child Behavioral Checklist (by Achenbach and Edelbrock) was developed in 1983 and is also widely used. It has a hyperactivity factor, but there is no factor related to distractibility.

New instruments have been developed that address the DSM-III-R criteria, including the Child Attention Problems (by Barkley), the ADHD Rating Scale (by DuPaul), and the Attention Deficit Disorders Evaluation Scale (by McCarney).

Teacher Rating Scales

Here again, the Conners series of teacher rating scales are the most widely used, and there are several versions. Likewise, the primary focus is on hyperactivity. The Conners Abbreviated Syndrome Questionnaire (by Conners and Barkley) is a ten-item list; however, it assesses general misconduct and aggression rather than inattention and other specific ADHD symptoms.

The Child Attention Problem rating scale (by Barkley) contains 12 items that specifically assess inattention and overactivity.

Newer Rating Instruments

The Yale Children's Inventory is a parent rating scale that assesses multiple factors related to ADHD and associated disorders. There are 11 scales: attention, impulsivity, activity, tractability, habituation, conduct disorder–socialized, conduct disorder–aggressive, negative affect, language, fine motor, and academics. With this scale an effort is made to identify hyperactivity, distractibility, and impulsivity, as well as evidence of an emotional disorder or learning difficulty.

❖ # Diagnosis of ADHD ❖

I have spent so much time telling you what ADHD is not, we should move on to what ADHD is. How is the diagnosis of ADHD established?

The clinical history and observational data best help the clinician establish the diagnosis of ADHD. The history is obtained from parents, teachers, school records, and other significant adults (such as scout leaders and religious educators). The observations should come from both the school and the home environment.

If the history of hyperactivity, distractibility, and/or impulsivity behaviors relate to specific times, spaces, or activities, anxiety might be the cause: "Billy was never hyperactive until third grade" or "Joan is only distractible in math class" or "Bob is only impulsive after his father gets home at night." These behaviors began at a certain point in the child's life or only appear to occur during specific times of the day.

If the history of these behaviors relates to a situational crisis or loss, depression might be the cause: "John was never hyperactive until his parents separated" or "Mary has become inattentive in class since her parents began openly fighting at home." Such behaviors might occur after obvious stresses such as parental fighting, separation, divorce, or the death of a family member. They might also occur after the birth of a sibling, moving to a new house, or starting in a new school. These behaviors have a clear starting point and appear to be related to a life stress.

If the behaviors began after entering a new environment, reaction to the environment might be the cause. Also, a learning disability and/or sensory integrative disorder should be excluded before the clinician concludes that the diagnosis is ADHD.

However, if these behaviors are *chronic* and *pervasive,* ADHD should be considered.

Chronic Behaviors

Chronic behaviors are those that have been present throughout the child's entire life. For example, your son's fourth-grade teacher might complain that he does not sit still or pay attention in class, and you find yourself thinking, "You think you have trouble, you should have heard his third-grade teacher and his second-grade teacher and his first-grade teacher and his kindergarten teacher. I have the only kid who was kicked out of nursery school because he would not sit still during circle time and pay attention." Or maybe you remember how he kicked more than usual in the womb, squirmed in your arms, and, in fact, has always been in motion: "He started to walk at ten months, and from ten months and one second on, he would run into another room, out the door, or into the street if I was not there to stop him" or "I can't remember one time in his whole life when he sat in his seat for an entire meal."

Pervasive Behaviors

Pervasive behaviors are those that are present all the time. You are not the only one who recognizes your child's hyperactivity, distractibility, and/or impulsivity. The classroom teacher describes these behaviors, as does the art teacher, the music teacher, the physical education teacher, and the lunchroom monitor. Even the Sunday School teacher, sports coach, and scout leader report the same behaviors.

❖ Summary ❖

Not all children and adolescents who show the behaviors of hyperactivity, distractibility, and/or impulsivity have ADHD. In reality, ADHD might be the least common cause for these behaviors. A clear differential diagnostic process that takes into account all possible causes for these behaviors is needed before a diagnosis is established. Because the diagnosis is made by a physician and some physicians may not be familiar with ADHD, you must be knowledgeable.

Once the diagnosis is established, it is important to explore the impact of ADHD on your child, as well as on the family. The behaviors will interfere with school performance. As you already know, the hyperactivity, distractibility, and/or impulsivity will interfere with family interactions and activities, as well as with peer relationships and activities. The treatment plan for ADHD is discussed in Chapter 9. It must take into account the total child or adolescent in his or her total environment. The treatment approach must go beyond prescribing medication.

If your child has been diagnosed as having ADHD only, it is critical that you consider whether he or she might also have a learning disability. There is an 80% likelihood that he or she does. If present, this disability must also be treated. The treatment for ADHD will not treat the learning disability, nor will the treatment for a learning disability treat the ADHD. Although associated, they are two different disorders.

If there are emotional, social, or family problems, the clinician must try to understand the role that ADHD and possible learning disabilities might play in causing or contributing to these problems. The treatment plan will be different if the emotional, social, or family problems are seen as the primary difficulty or if they are seen as secondary to the ADHD and possible learning disabilities and the impact these disabilities have had on the individual and family.

Associated Disorders

Chapter 4

Learning Disabilities

A s I discuss throughout this book, individuals with attention-deficit hyperactivity disorder (ADHD) may also have a learning disability. In addition, children and adolescents with a learning disability can show behaviors suggestive of ADHD. Thus it is important for you to understand learning disabilities. In my other book, *The Misunderstood Child: A Guide for Parents of Children With Learning Disabilities,* I go into much greater detail on learning disabilities and what parents can do to help their son or daughter with these disabilities (for more information, see Appendix A).

A not uncommon story I have heard from far too many parents goes like this:

A boy starts school and does not do well. By the third grade, he has not mastered basic skills, and he cannot stay on task or complete his assignments. The school decides the best approach is to hold him back. He is now a head taller and a year older than his classmates. His friends from the previous year move on and tease him about being kept back. By fifth grade, he is so far behind, he becomes increasingly frustrated, scared, and angry. He begins to misbehave in class. Throughout these years, his parents feel frustrated, worried, and helpless. The school staff call constantly to complain of his behavior or his incomplete work. More and more, the parents disagree on what to do. One believes the best way to raise their son is to be firm

41

and strict. The other believes that they should be understanding and permissive. Soon, they have marital problems. Finally, the principal calls the parents in and tells them their son is emotionally disturbed—probably because of the marital problems—and recommends they consult a child and adolescent psychiatrist or other mental health professional.

It is critical that this mental health professional sort out the cause from the consequence in this case. Is the principal correct that the boy has emotional problems, or might he have ADHD or a learning disability? Or might he have all of the above? If so, are the emotional and family problems causing the academic difficulties or are the emotional and family problems a consequence of the academic disabilities? Each conclusion leads to a very different treatment plan. These questions can only be answered with a knowledge of ADHD and learning disabilities. This chapter focuses on the question of learning disabilities.

❖ What Are Learning Disabilities? ❖ (Formal Definition)

Public schools use the definition of learning disabilities established by Federal Law: Education for All Handicapped Children (Public Law 94-142). This definition uses inclusionary and exclusionary criteria to define learning disabilities:

> "Specific learning disabilities" means a disorder in one or more of the basic psychological processes involved in understanding or in using language, spoken or written, which may manifest itself in an imperfect ability to listen, think, speak, read, write, spell, or to do mathematical calculations. The term includes such conditions as perceptual handicaps, brain injury, minimal brain dysfunction, dyslexia, and developmental aphasia. The term does not include children who have learning problems which are primarily the result of visual, hearing, or motor handicaps; of mental retardation; of emotional disturbance; or of environmental, cultural, or economic disadvantage.

Health and mental health professionals may use the definition found in their official diagnostic manual, the *Diagnostic and Statistical*

Manual of Mental Disorders, Third Edition, Revised (DSM-III-R). Because the terms used in DSM-III-R might be mentioned or written in a report, it is important for you to be familiar with them. These terms are different from those used by educational professionals (who used the terms in the Federal Law).

Rather than focus on the underlying learning disabilities, the concepts in DSM-III-R focus on the areas of academic difficulty, using the term *specific developmental disorders.* These disorders are broken into specific subcategories that focus on general areas of difficulty:

- Academic skills disorders
  - Developmental arithmetic disorder
  - Developmental expressive writing disorder
  - Developmental reading disorder
- Language and speech disorders
  - Developmental articulation disorder
  - Developmental expressive language disorder
  - Developmental receptive language disorder
- Motor skills disorder
  - Developmental coordination disorder

These specific developmental disorders are described as "inadequate development of specific academic, language, speech, and motor skills that are not due to demonstrable physical or neurological disorders, [major psychiatric disorders], mental retardation, or deficient educational opportunities."

DSM-III-R differs significantly from federal and state classification systems for children and adolescents with learning disabilities. The latter systems state in their definition that such individuals are of at least average intelligence. In DSM-III-R, a child who is performing academic skills below his or her intellectual potential is diagnosed as having an academic skills disorder even if he or she is mentally retarded.

When working in or with a school system, the term *learning disabilities* will be used. When completing medical or insurance forms, mental health professionals will use DSM-III-R terminology. Regardless of the label used, the primary concern must be an awareness of such a disability.

❖ What Are Learning Disabilities? ❖ (Clinical Definition)

Most educational test instruments and special educational literature use a computer-based or cybernetics model for understanding learning and learning disabilities. It is understood that any learning task involves more than one process and that any learning disability can involve more than one area of dysfunction. However, breaking learning down into steps helps to clarify the process.

The first step in this model is *input,* in which information enters the brain from the sense organs. Once the information is recorded, it is processed and interpreted, a process called *integration.* Next, the information must be used or stored and later retrieved, the *memory* process. Finally, this information must be sent out through language or muscle activities, the *output* process. It is important to understand this input → integration → memory → output process, as well as the terminology and concepts used by professionals in the field of learning disabilities.

Input Disabilities

Input is a process of the central brain and does not pertain to peripheral visual or auditory problems. We refer to this process of perceiving our environment as *perception.* A child might have a visual or an auditory perception disability, as well as perception disabilities related to sensory integration or taste and smell.

Visual perception disability. Children with visual perception disability have difficulty organizing the position and shape of what they see. Input may be perceived with letters and numbers reversed or rotated: an *n* might look like a *u;* an *E* might look like a *3,* a *W,* or an *M.* The letters *d, b, p,* and *q* might be confused with each other. This confusion with position of input is normal until about age five or six. It becomes apparent when these children begin to copy letters or designs or to read or write.

Other children might have a *figure-ground* problem; that is, they have difficulty focusing on the significant figure instead of the other visual inputs in the background. Reading requires this skill, focusing on specific letters or groups of letters, then tracking from left to right, line after line. When reading, children with this disability may skip over words, read the same line twice, or skip lines.

Judging distances or depth perception is another visual perception task that can be dysfunctional. Some children may misjudge depth, bumping into things, falling off a chair, or knocking over a drink because their hand reaches the glass sooner than expected.

Auditory perception disabilities. Children may also have difficulty with one of several aspects of auditory perception. Children who have difficulty distinguishing subtle differences in sounds will misunderstand what is said and may respond incorrectly. Words that sound alike are often confused—*blue* with *blow, ball* with *bell,* or *can* with *can't.* A boy with this disability who is asked "How are you?" might answer "I'm nine years old," thinking that he heard "old" instead of "are" or in addition to "are."

Some children have difficulty with auditory figure-ground. They might be watching television in a room where others are playing or talking, and a parent or teacher may call out to speak to them, but it might not be until the third paragraph verbalized that they begin to pick the voice (figure) out of the other sound inputs (background). To those around them, it appears that these children never listen or pay attention.

Some children cannot process sound inputs as quickly as most other people can. This problem is called an *auditory lag.* Listening to a normal rate of speech, such children need to focus on each thought they hear for a fraction of a second longer than most people do to understand. Therefore, they must concentrate on what was just heard while trying to hold on to what is coming in next. Gradually, they get behind and must jump ahead to what is currently being said, and so part of what is being said is missed. For example, a teacher explains a math problem. A child with auditory lag hears and understands steps one, two, and three, then misses step four, picks up again with step five, and is lost and confused. To parents or teachers talking to this child, he or she appears not to be paying attention or not to understand what is being said.

Sensory integrative disorder. Several other sensory inputs are critical to understanding our environment. These inputs are needed to orient our bodies in space and to move them in space. There is currently a debate as to whether these sensory input difficulties result in a learning disability. There is no debate that they interfere with awareness of the body and of body movement and, thus, that they are a life disability. These sensory inputs relate to touch (tactile perception), muscle and joint activity (proprioception perception), and head position and gravity (vestibular perception).

Children with *tactile perception* difficulties confuse input from the nerve endings in their skin for light touch and for deep touch, that is, the degree of pressure. They may be tactilely defensive (from early childhood they will not like being touched or held). They are sensitive to touch and may perceive it as uncomfortable. Often they complain of the tag on the back of a shirt, their belt being too tight, or their clothes feeling funny. Parents learn that deep touch is tolerated better and may calm the child down.

Some children with tactile sensitivity are defensive and try to avoid body contact. For example, a boy with tactile sensitivity might be walking down the hall, and another child lightly brushes against him. He might respond as if the touch was a major blow and hit the other child. Other children may experience touch deprivation and the need for body contact; they might walk around the room touching other children to the annoyance of the children and the teacher.

Joint position, muscle tone, movement, and body position are perceived through *proprioception perception*. These inputs help to develop muscle tone, and information from the muscles is used to hold a body upright or to hold, push, pull, and carry. Children and adolescents having difficulty with this sensory input may be confused with their body in space and may have difficulty with muscle tone and postural mechanisms; thus they will have difficulty changing the body to keep from losing their balance. They may have difficulty with motor planning and with the coordinated use of muscles in activities such as buttoning and tying. Some children with this disability experience a proprioception deprivation; they might like to stomp their feet or bump into walls.

Vestibular perception tells the brain where the body is in space (upside down, lying on stomach, lying on back, etc.) and how it is moving (fast, slow, around, forward, backward, etc.). Unclear vestibular perception may make it difficult for children or adolescents to interact with gravity and sense body movement in space, particularly changes in the position of their head. Some children may experience vestibular deprivation and enjoy spinning in chairs or on swings.

Depending on which sensory systems are involved in the sensory integrative disorder, children and adolescents may have problems with tactile sensitivity, coordinating body movements, and adapting to the position of the body in space. In addition, they may have difficulty with motor planning, that is, the ability to easily direct their body to perform activities in a smooth, coordinated manner.

Taste and smell.   No research to date has explored whether taste and smell inputs might be dysfunctional with children and adolescents who have a learning disability. However, because these children have difficulties with the other sensory systems, it is possible that these systems might also be involved.

I have had parents tell me that their child's taste is supersensitive, that he or she does not like certain foods because they "taste funny" or "feel funny in my mouth." Other parents report that their child smells things that they do not; these children seem to be very sensitive to smells or smell things differently.

Integration Disabilities

Once information enters the brain, it has to be understood. At least three steps are required to do this: *sequencing, abstraction,* and *organization.* Children and adolescents can have disabilities in any or in all of these areas. If the disability in sequencing relates to visual input, it is called a *visual sequencing disability.* If the difficulty lies with auditory input, it is called an *auditory sequencing disability.* So, too, children might have difficulty with *visual abstraction* or with *auditory abstraction.* Organization difficulties usually involve all areas of input.

Sequencing disabilities.   Children with a sequencing disability might hear or read a story, but, in recounting it, they start in the middle, go to the beginning, and then shift to the end. Eventually the whole story comes out, but the sequence of events is wrong. They might have the same difficulty in writing. All of the information is written but in the wrong order. Or they might see the word *dog* and read it as "god." Spelling words with all of the right letters in the wrong order also can reflect this disability.

These children might have difficulty using a sequence of facts. They might memorize a sequence, such as the days of the week or the months of the year, but they are unable to use single units out of the sequence correctly. Asked what comes after August, the children cannot answer spontaneously, but must go back over the whole sequence, "January, February, March . . ." before they can answer. These children might know the alphabet, but they cannot use the dictionary without continuously starting at the letter *a* and then working up to the letter used.

Abstraction disabilities.   After information is recorded in the brain and placed in the right sequence, its meaning must be inferred. Most children with learning disabilities have only minor difficulties in this area. Abstraction, the ability to derive the correct general meaning from a particular word or symbol, is a very basic intellectual task. If the disability in this area is too great, the child is apt to be functioning at a retarded level.

Some children, however, do have more subtle problems with abstraction. For example, a teacher reads a story about a police officer to a group of second or third graders and then begins a discussion about police officers in general. The teacher asks the students whether they know any men or women in their neighborhood who are police officers and, if so, what they do. Children with an abstraction disability may not be able to answer the question. They can only talk about the particular officer in the story and not about police officers in general. Older children with an abstraction disability might have difficulty understanding jokes since much of humor is based on plays on words, which confuse them. Likewise, they might have difficulty with idioms or puns. These children often take what is said literally and may appear to be paranoid.

Organization disabilities. Once recorded, sequenced, and under-stood, new information must be integrated with a constant flow of data and then related to previously learned information. Some children have difficulty pulling together multiple parts of information into a full or complete concept. These children may learn a series of facts but are not able to answer general questions that require using these facts. Their notes, reports, desks, and lockers may be disorganized. They may leave work needed at home in school or work needed in school at home. They have problems organizing and planning their time. Their rooms at home may be disorganized, as well.

Memory Disabilities

After information is received, recorded in the brain, and integrated, it has to be stored so that it can be retrieved later. There are two types of this storage and retrieval process (or memory): short-term and long-term.

Short-term memory is the process of retaining information for a brief time while attending to or concentrating on it. For example, after calling the information operator for a long-distance phone number, most people can retain the ten digits long enough to dial the number if it is done right away. However, if someone starts talking to them in the course of dialing, they may forget the number. *Long-term memory* is the process of storing information that has been repeated often enough that it can be retained and retrieved by thinking of it.

Most children with a memory disability have a short-term disability. Like abstraction disability, a long-term memory disability interferes so much with functioning that children with this disability are more likely to be functioning as retarded. A child with a short-term memory prob-lem may require many more repetitions to retain what the average child retains after a few repetitions. Yet, the same child usually has no problem with long-term memory, surprising parents with details from years ago.

A short-term memory disability can occur with information re-ceived visually (a *visual short-term memory disability*) or with infor-mation received auditorily (an *auditory short-term memory disability*). Often the two are combined. For example, the child might review a spelling list one evening and know it well while he or she is concentrating on it, but in school the next day it is forgotten. Or a teacher might go over a math concept in class until it is understood, but the child forgets how to do the problems at home that night. Likewise, some children stop midway through what they are saying and say, "Oh, forget it" or "Never mind" because they forgot what they were saying. They use these statements to cover up their short-term memory problem.

Some children and adolescents have difficulty retaining what they read. This problem also might be a reflection of a short-term memory disability. They read the first paragraph and understand it. They read the second paragraph and understand it. They read the third, fourth, and other paragraphs and understand each. Yet, when they get to the end of the chapter, they have forgotten what they read.

Output Disabilities

Information is expressed through spoken words (language output) or through muscle activity such as writing, drawing, and gesturing (motor output). Children and adolescents may have a *language disability* or a *motor disability.*

Language disabilities. Two forms of language are used in communication: spontaneous language and demand language. In spontaneous language, the individual initiates what is said. He or she has the opportunity to select the subject, organize his or her thoughts, and find the correct words before speaking. In demand language, someone else sets up a circumstance (asking a question, for example), and the individual must simultaneously organize, find the correct words, and speak.

Children with a language disability usually have no difficulty with spontaneous language; they may, however, have problems with demand language. The inconsistency can be quite striking. A child with demand language problems may initiate all sorts of conversation, may never keep quiet in fact, and may sound very normal. However, put in a situation that demands a response, the same child might answer, "Huh?" or "What?" or "I don't know." Or he or she may ask you to repeat the question to gain time, or may not answer at all. If the child is forced to answer, the response may be so confusing or circumstantial that it is difficult to follow. He or she may sound totally unlike the child who was speaking so fluently just a moment ago.

Motor disabilities. Difficulty coordinating groups of large muscles, such as those in the limbs or trunk, is called a *gross motor disability*. Difficulty in performing tasks that require coordination of groups of small muscles is called a *fine motor disability*.

Gross motor disabilities may cause children to be clumsy, stumble, fall, bump into things, or have difficulty with generalized physical activities like running, climbing, or swimming. They might have difficulty with buttoning, zipping, or tying.

The most common form of a fine motor disability is difficulty with writing. The problem lies, in part, in an inability to get the many small muscles in the dominant hand to work together as a team. Children with this "written language" disability have slow, poor handwriting. They complain, "My hand does not work as fast as my head is thinking." In addition to the mechanical aspect of writing, such children may have difficulty with the flow of thoughts through the muscles onto the page. They might make spelling, grammar, or punctuation errors or write with poor syntax.

If a child has a visual perception disability and, thus, provides incorrect information for the brain to use in doing motor tasks, he or she will have eye-hand coordination difficulties. For example, a child might have difficulty coloring and staying in the lines, cutting and staying on the line, or catching a ball. Children with these difficulties have a *visual motor disability*.

The Learning Disability Profile

Obviously, the learning process is much more complex; however, this simple model for describing specific learning disabilities can be helpful. Each individual with a learning disability will have his or her profile of learning abilities and learning disabilities. There is no set pattern of learning disabilities. Each child and adolescent must be evaluated and understood differently. This information is essential for understanding the individual and for planning the appropriate educational and/or clinical interventions.

❖ **Clues That Might Suggest** ❖
a Learning Disability

When a clinician evaluates a child or adolescent with emotional or behavioral problems associated with poor academic performance, he or she must consider the possibility of ADHD and/or of a learning disability. As a parent you will be asked to provide a history of school experiences, starting with preschool. The clinician will ask you questions like "Has your child had difficulty year after year?" or "Have teachers described your child as hyperactive or distractible in each grade?" or "Has your child had academic problems every year?"

Your child can be of help. Knowing the input → integration → memory → output model, both you, as a parent, and the clinician can ask your child questions about school performance. The questions flow from the model:

- Reading
  - How well do you read? Do you like to read?
  - When you read, do you make silly mistakes like skipping words or lines or reading the same lines twice?
  - Do you find that you can read each line or paragraph but that when you finish the page or chapter you don't remember what you've read?
- Writing
  - How is your handwriting?
  - Do you find that you can't write as fast as you are thinking? If so, do you overlap words because you are thinking of the next word but writing another?
  - How is your spelling? grammar? punctuation?
  - Do you have difficulty copying off of the blackboard?
- Math
  - Do you know your times tables?
  - When you do math do you make silly mistakes like write "21"

when you mean to write "12," or do you mix up your columns or add when you mean to subtract?

■ Do you sometimes start a math problem but halfway through forget what you are trying to do?

Other questions can focus on areas not covered under the review of specific skills:

■ Sequencing
  ■ When you speak or write, do you sometimes have difficulty getting everything in the right order, maybe starting in the middle, going to the beginning, then jumping to the end?
  ■ Can you tell me the months of the year? Fine, now what comes after August? (Once answered, ask how he or she got the answer.)
  ■ Do you have trouble using the alphabet in order? Do you have to start from the beginning each time?
■ Abstraction
  ■ Do you understand jokes when your friends tell them?
  ■ Do you sometimes get confused when people seem to say something, yet they tell you they meant something else?
■ Organization
  ■ What does your notebook look like? Is it a mess with papers in the wrong place or falling out? What about your desk? Your locker?
  ■ Do you sometimes have difficulty organizing your thoughts or the facts you are learning into a whole concept so that you can learn it?
  ■ Do you find that you can read a chapter and answer the questions at the end of the chapter but that you are still not sure what the chapter was about?
  ■ Do you have trouble planning your time so that things get done on time?
  ■ What does your room at home look like?
■ Memory
  ■ Do you find that you can learn something at night and then go to school the next day and forget what you have learned?

- When talking, do you sometimes know what you want to say but halfway through you forget what you are saying? If so, do you cover up by saying things like "Oh, forget it" or "It's not important"?
- Language
  - When the teacher is speaking in class, do you have trouble understanding or keeping up?
  - Do you sometimes misunderstand people and, thus, give the wrong answer?
  - When people are talking do you find that you have to concentrate on what they say so hard that you sometimes fall behind and have to skip quickly to what they are now saying to keep up? Does this sometimes cause you to get lost in class?
  - Do you sometimes have trouble getting your thoughts organized when you speak? Do you have a problem finding the word you want to use?

Often when I go over these questions with children or adolescents, they look amazed and ask me if I could read their mind. How could I have known about their problems? Sometimes they did not understand their problems until they had to explain them to me.

During the diagnostic sessions, the clinician might pick up other clues of a learning disability. The child or adolescent might have difficulty with listening and understanding what the clinician says or with expressing himself or herself clearly. The child might have difficulty doing activities requiring visual perception or visual motor tasks or playing a game that requires reading, counting, or following a sequence.

❖ **Learning Disabilities** ❖
Are Life Disabilities

Learning disabilities do not just interfere with reading, writing, or math. They also interfere with baseball, basketball, four square, hopscotch, jump rope, dressing, setting the dinner table, and making small talk. As a parent, you and your child can provide clues from activities outside the classroom that might suggest a learning disability. Let me illustrate, using the input → integration → memory → output model.

Input Disabilities

A child or adolescent with visual perception difficulties may have problems with sports requiring catching, throwing, or hitting a ball. These motor tasks require visual figure-ground ability to spot the ball and depth perception ability to track the ball, as well as visual motor ability to convert the input information into getting the body and arms to the right place at the right time.

Children with depth perception problems may fall off of their seats, bump into things, or misjudge the distance to a drink and knock over the glass. Some may be confused by large, open spaces such as gyms or shopping malls. Some children with this problem may develop an anxiety disorder or panic disorder related to open spaces.

Individuals with an auditory perception problem might misunderstand what adults or peers say and thus respond incorrectly. Some may have difficulty knowing what sounds to listen to. They might miss what is being said to them by parents or friends because they were listening to one sound and did not realize that another sound had started. Some may have a delay in processing speech. They appear to be not listening or to be staring into space; they might be called an "air head" or "space cadet."

Less is known about other sensory inputs. Infants and children may be tactilely defensive or confused or uncomfortable with touch. Some complain of clothes being too tight or of certain materials feeling uncomfortable. Some children seem hypersensitive to smell, complaining that things or places "smell funny." Others may have oversensitive taste.

We know little about the effect of perception problems during infancy. If such disabilities are apparent with young children, might not they be present from birth? How would they impact on early interactions or on bonding if the infant misperceived sounds, visions, smells, or touch? Could these difficulties explain in part the frequent complaint that a child had difficulty with eating, sleeping, and being calmed from the earliest weeks of life?

Integration Disabilities

Children or adolescents with sequencing problems may confuse the steps involved in playing a game or might hit the ball and run to third base rather than to first. Young children might have difficulty dressing, putting their pants on before their underpants. Such children might also have difficulty following directions or making the bed, building models, or setting the dinner table properly.

Much of humor is based on subtle changes in the meaning of words or phrases. Individuals with difficulty with abstraction may miss the meaning of jokes and be out of place with peers. They might have difficulty with slang expressions. Some will appear to be paranoid because they misinterpret words or actions or interpret them more concretely. Organizational problems may be reflected in a disorganized room or notebook or in an inability to plan their time or carry out activities. Parents and friends may complain that such persons can't get their act together.

Memory Disabilities

Children and adolescents with a memory disability might meet someone they have known for a long time but not remember his or her name. Or a parent might ask a child to go into the garage and get the hammer, some nails, and a ruler, and the child returns with only the hammer. Parents of children with memory disabilities say that they cannot give more than one instruction at a time. These children also frustrate their parents and friends because they stop in the middle of what they are saying and say, "Oh, forget it."

Output Disabilities

The inability to write quickly and legibly or to spell can be a problem with games, activities, taking telephone messages, or writing a note to a friend. Mistakes are laughed at or associated with not being smart. Motor coordination difficulties can cause problems with buttoning, zipping, playing games, cutting up food, or playing sports. Because success in sports is such a major part of childhood peer acceptance, difficulties with motor coordination can be a major social handicap.

Expressive language problems make communication difficult with peers, siblings, and adults. Children with such difficulties will have problems with small talk or with interacting in a conversation. Often they become shy and avoid talking or being with people for fear that they will say the wrong thing and appear to be foolish.

❖ Establishing the Diagnosis ❖ of a Learning Disability

If you suspect your child has a learning disability, discuss your concerns with the classroom teacher and the principal. Each school system has a different process for requesting a formal evaluation for learning disabilities. Your legal rights as a parent are discussed in Chapter 16.

You might also discuss your concerns with your family physician. If, based on a medical evaluation, the family and/or school history, and the clinical and observational data, your family physician agrees there is a possibility of a learning disability, he or she could assist you in getting your school system to do the necessary studies or could refer you to a private source.

The diagnosis of a learning disability is confirmed through psychological and educational testing. These tests might be done by one person or by a diagnostic team. This "psychoeducational" evaluation assesses three areas: 1) the child's intellectual potential and cognitive style, 2) his or her level of academic skills, and 3) evidence of a specific learning disability.

The psychological assessment may consist of a neuropsychological or a clinical-psychological evaluation. IQ test results can help determine whether there are any discrepancies between a child's verbal and performance abilities or between the individual subtest scores on formal tests of intellectual assessment. Other psychological tests will assess perception, cognitive, and language abilities. The educational diagnostician or the psychologist will measure the child's current level of academic skills using standard achievement tests. If the results of these more general studies suggest the child might have a learning disability, he or she will be evaluated further, using more specific tests, such as the Woodcock-Johnson Psychoeducational Battery.

If the child has disabilities in the motor areas, an occupational therapist might do further studies. For language disabilities, a speech and language therapist might assess the child in greater detail. Other professionals might be included as part of the diagnostic team if the initial studies suggest other specific problem areas (such as audiology or neurology).

The results of these evaluations should establish the presence or absence of a learning disability. If present, the results will clarify also the specific areas of learning disability as well as of learning ability. The observational data plus test results might suggest hyperactivity, distractibility, and/or impulsivity.

❖ Treatment for Learning Disabilities ❖

The treatment of choice for learning disabilities in school is special education. Professionals trained in this area work on helping the child to overcome the learning disabilities and to compensate for those disabilities that cannot be overcome. Strategies for learning are taught based on the child's areas of strengths and weaknesses. The classroom teacher must learn to build on the child's strengths in the classroom while helping to accommodate for the weaknesses.

The treatment of choice for learning disabilities outside of school is educating the parents and the child. They must learn to build on strengths while understanding and adapting or accommodating for the weaknesses. They must use this knowledge to select chores, activities, sports, or camps that are most likely to be successful.

My book, *The Misunderstood Child: A Guide for Parents of Children with Learning Disabilities,* expands on these concepts (see Appendix A). It is written primarily for parents and discusses how they can build on their son's or daughter's strengths rather than magnify their weaknesses as they try to help their child and their family.

❖ Summary ❖

Learning disabilities and ADHD are related, but different, disorders. A child who cannot sit still or who is distracted and who cannot stay on task will have difficulty learning. It is important to differentiate whether this child has ADHD, a learning disability, or both.

It is important for you as a parent to suspect a learning disability if your son or daughter has school, academic, and behavioral problems. The child with learning difficulties solely may be referred for a psychoeducational evaluation. The child with behavioral or emotional problems may be referred to the family physician, pediatrician, child and adolescent psychiatrist, or another mental health professional. Each professional must look for the possibility of ADHD as well as of a learning disability. If there are emotional or behavioral problems, the clinician must determine whether they are the cause of or the consequence of the academic difficulties.

Treatment interventions will be based on the child's diagnostic profile. The treatment for a learning disability will not treat ADHD, nor will the treatment for ADHD treat a learning disability. Further, a primary focus on the emotional or behavioral problems without addressing the underlying causes for these problems will be less than successful.

Chapter 5

Normal Psychosocial Development

Before I can discuss the emotional and social problems of children and adolescents with attention-deficit hyperactivity disorder (ADHD), it is necessary for you, the parent, to know about normal psychological and social development. Only with this knowledge and reference can you understand the difficulties your son or daughter might experience.

Not long ago, a mother called me about her son. "He refuses to leave me," she said. "He clings to me and cries if I try to walk away. If I leave him with someone else, he throws a tantrum. What should I do with him?" I couldn't advise anything until I found out her son's age. If he were one year old, this could be quite normal. If he were two, I would be slightly worried. If he were four or eight, I would be very concerned. If he were 15, I would be alarmed. "Normal" behavior has a great deal to do with a child's age and the stage of development he or she is in at the time.

All children go through stages of psychological and social development, and most do so with minimal difficulty. They may occasionally face a stressful situation—being in the hospital, getting used to a new baby brother or sister, or coping with their parents' divorce—and briefly retreat back to earlier behaviors, but ordinarily they soon rally and move ahead again. Growth means many steps forward with occasional steps backward.

Much of this psychological and social (or psychosocial) growth interweaves with stages in physical growth. As the brain and body mature, the child develops new abilities with which to handle problems. This same growth, however, also introduces new problems.

Most children go through the various stages of development without serious difficulties. Some children, however, will have difficulty going through these stages. Likewise, some children and families find certain stages of growth more difficult than others.

❖ Normal Child Development ❖

Newborn infants function primarily as physiological beings, their brain receiving messages from their body and sending messages to the body to respond. During the early weeks and months, babies begin to become conscious of certain significant people, recognizing their mother's or father's voice, image, or smell, for example. As infants begin to relate to their world, they are unaware of any distinction between their bodies and things in their environment; they have no sense of boundaries. People, pets, food, furniture, favorite toys, all objects outside of the self appear to be merely extensions of the self. Significant parenting people are there, but not uniquely related to.

This stage of development looks something like this

Figure 1

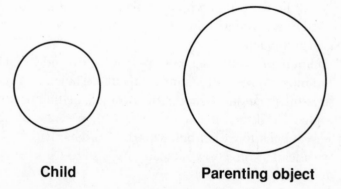

Child   Parenting object

Basic Trust

Gradually infants begin to discover that things have extensions and limits to them as well. They discover their fingers, hands, toes, and feet and find that these objects belong to the same body that they have begun to experience. By about three months they can recognize certain pieces of the external world, and they relate to these "part objects" in special ways that acknowledge their importance. Now we see for the first time the "social smile." Infants look at a part of a face and smile. This social smile is an early psychological landmark of normal development.

By about nine months, most infants have completed the process of discovering where they leave off and the world begins. They have discovered that there are many human objects in the world. Having learned to associate pleasurable experiences with certain human objects, they begin to comprehend that these specific human objects are very important—that they are absolutely necessary, in fact. Thus infants learn to place a *basic trust* in these key people, and they become *totally dependent* on them.

With the establishment of basic trust, infants master the first major step in psychosocial development. But now they become upset if left alone. They fear separation and strangers. Before this stage, anyone could pick them up and get a smile. Now if someone unknown or not very well known picks them up, they start to cry. This fear, which normally appears at around nine months, is another psychosocial landmark. The infant becomes totally dependent on the parent.

This stage of total dependency might look like this

Figure 2

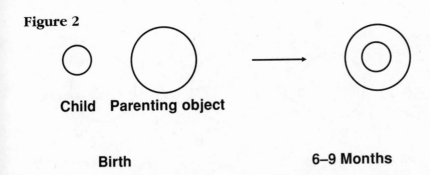

Child   Parenting object

Birth   6–9 Months

Separation

The next task in psychosocial development is separation. Infants must realize that they can separate from these significant people and still survive and then learn how to do that. Mastery of this stage of development involves several steps, which start at about nine to 12 months and usually finish at three to three-and-a-half years. This accomplishment of separation, which leads to a sense of an autonomous self, is illustrated in Figure 3.

Initially (see *a* in Figure 3), infants must have some form of sensory connection with the significant person. They cry, they hear a parent's footsteps in the hall, and then they stop crying. This auditory linkage is enough. Or they crawl behind a chair, lose sight of their parent, and start to cry. When the parent moves into view, they stop. This visual link, the sight of the parent, reestablishes the necessary contact. Babies cry at night. When their mother or father picks them up in the dark and holds them, they stop crying. The touch, smell, and voice of the parent reassure them that the intimate connection is not broken.

Beginning at about 18 to 24 months, children slowly learn to separate for longer and longer periods of time (see *b* in Figure 3). Yet toddlers still must return frequently to the parent to "refuel" or "tag up." A hug, a kiss, or a cookie will do, and they are off again. Some children find these early efforts at separating easier if they can take something that reminds them of a parent along with them. Children usually select these favorite things (which we commonly call "security blankets" but are more properly called "transitional objects") because they have a familiar smell, soft touch, or cuddly feel that the children have learned to associate with the parent.

Figure 3

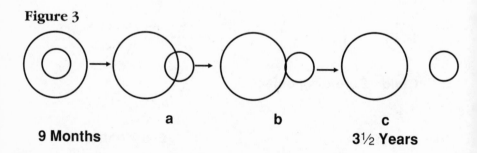

a   b   c

9 Months   3½ Years

By about three to three-and-a-half years, children can finally separate from their parents with no discomfort (see *c* in Figure 3). This full mastery of separation is yet another landmark in psychosocial development.

Two major psychological events take place during this stage, one internally motivated, the other externally caused. Each aids in mastering separation and in establishing autonomy, and each has a major influence on personality development. The internal event is *negativism,* and this begins at about age two. During the "terrible twos," children respond to most requests or comments with "No" or "No, I do myself." They are beginning to separate and to show that they have a mind of their own. Although exasperating to parents, this healthy step toward separation and autonomy is a very necessary one.

The external event, which occurs at about age two, is *toilet training.* In learning to accede to this requirement of the outside world, children confront two new tasks that have to be mastered. First, they must alter their concept of love and relationships. Until now they have perceived the whole world as being there to take care of them. Love and caring were automatic and free. Suddenly they face a situation in which love is no longer free and available on demand. Now if they want love, they must do something to get it. Loving relationships no longer center totally around their wishes and needs; now they must learn to participate in a give-and-take process. Urinate in the potty and Mommy loves you; urinate in your pants and Mommy frowns or spanks or threatens not to like you. Getting love sometimes requires doing what is wanted, that is, what is lovable. To receive pleasure requires pleasing. This forces children to make a revolutionary shift in their concept of the world, of people, and of relationships.

Toilet training introduces a second new concept that provides children with a new way to handle angry feelings. For the first time they have an active weapon in the battle to get what they want. Before this, they could cry or have a tantrum, but the parents could choose to ignore it. Before this, they experienced anger and expressed it openly by crying, screaming, kicking, or hitting. Now they begin to realize that there are different ways to express anger and that the way they express anger has a great deal to do with getting and keeping love. Direct expressions of anger don't work. The price they have to pay may be too great. Children now learn that more indirect expressions of anger work somewhat better than hitting and yelling. Now when angry with their parents, they can squat right in front of them, preferably when company is around, and, with a big smile, "make" in their pants. If they are pleased with Mommy and Daddy, they will "make" on the potty. They begin to learn the importance of controlling anger or, more precisely, of learning subtler, more ambiguous, and therefore more acceptable ways to express anger.

These issues—the reciprocal nature of loving and being loved, pleasing and being pleased, and handling angry feelings—are struggled with individually and together. The two themes often interrelate: at this age children can readily love and hate the same person at the same time or hurt and care for the same person at the same time.

Individuation

When a child has mastered the first major task of development, establishing basic trust, and the second major task, handling separation, he or she is ready for the third task, *individuation.* This task involves asking and trying to answer the question "Who am I?" Now that the child knows that he or she is a separate person who can survive without being totally dependent on important people, what kind of person is that child? The struggle to answer these questions usually takes place between the ages of three and six.

During this stage, the brain is still immature, and not all thinking is based on reality. Fantasy, which seems as real as what is real, forms one basis for a lot of the thinking children do. If they think something is so, it may as well be so. Thus children at this age can have opposite beliefs and feelings simultaneously, with no notion that a contradiction exists or that only one of two or more different possibilities can come true. Loving and hating, wanting and not wanting, going to a movie and going on a picnic at the same time—children exclude nothing and see no problem with believing in all possibilities coming true at the same time.

Children also try out many roles. If they pretend to be Superman, they *are* Superman. What is it like to be big? Little? Aggressive? Submissive? A boy? A girl? Children play "house" or "school" or "doctor," exploring various roles and different situations. One day your daughter may act like a boy, the next day a girl, or a Mommy, a Daddy, a teacher, a gangster, ET, or Miss Piggy. Your daughter or son tries to learn about people and how to do things and tries to master those concerns through repetition in play. For example, children must learn to listen to adults other than their parents. When they play school, they take turns being the teacher who gives instructions and orders and then the pupil who must listen and obey. When they play doctor, they take turns being the doctor who explores and the patient who is explored.

Whenever children try to "be" someone else in the family, mother or father, for instance, they have to compete with that person for her or his identity and roles, as well as with any sibling who may also want to be that parent. They also have to try to attract the attention of the other parent. So another characteristic of this age period is the tendency of children to cause parents to disagree and, thus, cause tension between their parents as well as among their siblings. Children learn with remarkable aptitude how to divide parents, getting one closer to them and pushing the other away. Thus on one day they may seem close and loving, yet on another day they are irritating and hostile.

For the first time, our diagram of the child's relationships must include both parents (*M*, mother; *F*, father), as illustrated here

Figure 4

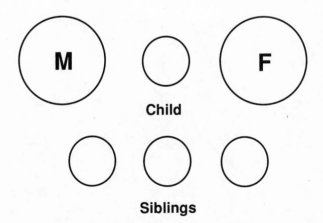

67

If the boy or girl wants to play "being mother," then mother must be pushed away, along with any siblings who might compete for her role, as illustrated here

Figure 5

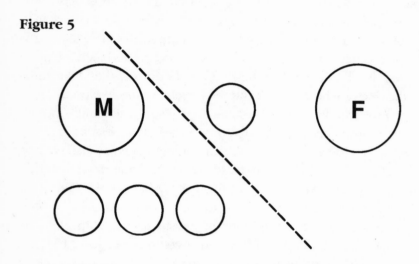

Likewise, if the child wants to play "being father," then father has to be pushed away, along with any siblings who might want that role, as illustrated here

Figure 6

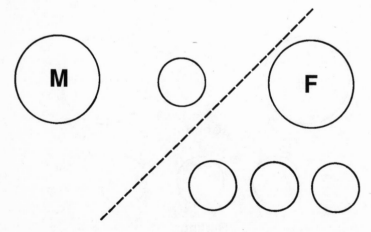

Because both splits occur from time to time, our overall diagram has to look like this

Figure 7

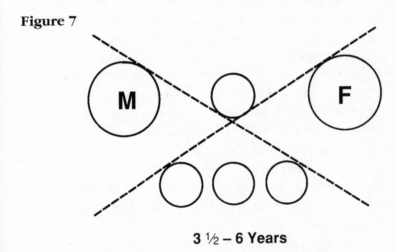

3 ½ – 6 Years

The thinking of children at this age is magical (that is, it is not based on reality), and they have trouble distinguishing among what actually are feelings, thoughts, and actions. Their thoughts, especially their angry thoughts, scare them. Nightmares are common. Children worry that others, like their parents, know what they are thinking and that they will retaliate. This magical fear of retaliation causes children to worry excessively about body integrity and body damage. Any cut or scratch is a disaster. This is why this age is often called the "Band-Aid" stage.

During these frustrating fours and fives, most children and their parents do have a lot of fun. Children this age are animated, uninhibited, and imaginative, and they enjoy interacting and playing. On the other hand, these children can cause stress between parents and among siblings. In addition, they may have trouble sleeping, having nightmares and wanting to sleep with the parents. One minute you love and cuddle the child, the next you feel like giving him or her away to the nearest stranger. All of this is normal.

By about age six, most children begin to find preliminary answers to the question "Who am I?" Little girls begin to learn that they are to become "just like Mommy" and enjoy playing this role. They give up wanting Daddy all to themselves and look forward to some day having someone just like their father. Likewise, little boys begin to learn that they are to become "just like Daddy"; they give up wanting Mommy all to themselves and settle for the idea of having someone just like their mother some day ("I want a girl just like the girl that married dear old dad"). Although some of these self-assessments may later change, it is through this process of identification that children learn to become more or less like the parent of the same sex. (The child in a single-parent family may have more difficulty working through this stage of development. Most make it through, but if you think that consulting a mental health professional would help, don't hesitate to get advice for yourself and, perhaps, help for your child.)

Between ages three and six, most children are struggling to establish basic assumptions about their identities. During this time, parents are also doing their imprinting of stereotypical sex-role behaviors. If a boy reaches for a doll to play with, he is brusquely told that boys play with trucks or guns, not with dolls. Many parents teach their little girls that they play with dolls and do things in the kitchen, that they do not work with tools or guns or trucks. Girls are taught that it is acceptable to express love and sadness but not self-assertion or anger. Boys learn that it is acceptable to express anger but that "big boys don't cry."

Fortunately, the consciousness-raising efforts of the women's movement have helped to free more and more families from the need to pass along these stereotypes. Children must feel free to explore and to learn many roles in becoming fully developed males or females. They must learn that true maleness and femaleness has nothing to do with the things one does or how one expresses different emotions, but with the kinds of resources and experiences one has, the kinds of relationships one can sustain, and the respect one develops toward oneself and others.

Toward the end of this stage, at about age six, two changes take place that help children master the process of individuation. The first change is that the central nervous system takes a large maturational leap forward, and this helps children move from nonreality-based thinking to reality-based thinking. Contradictory feelings and thoughts can no longer coexist with equal power. Children begin to understand that feeling or thinking one thing means that they cannot believe in its opposite at the same time with equal conviction. In other words, the realization dawns that they cannot do or be two (or more) things at the same time. Children can now distinguish between reality and fantasy. They may pretend to be Superman, but they know it is only pretend.

The second change involves children's emerging awareness of the various accumulated values and value judgments they have learned. At about this age, these fuse into an established conscience, called the *superego*. This conscience or "voice," stays with them throughout their life and becomes increasingly significant. It "tells" them which thoughts, feelings, and actions are acceptable and which are not. Initially, parents teach these values, and children usually adopt them fairly automatically. They may rebel at this age, but that is more because they want to do what they want to do, not because they have serious questions about moral or intellectual validity. In adolescence, as we shall see, these values are routinely reviewed and reconsidered.

Latency

Once children master the third task of development, individuation, they move into a period of consolidation. Sometime around age six, children become free to move out of the family and into the community. With the major psychological work of childhood done, their energy is freed to range more widely in school and other learning activities and in expanding relationships. This period, which lasts about six to eight years, is called the *latency* period and can be illustrated like this

Figure 8

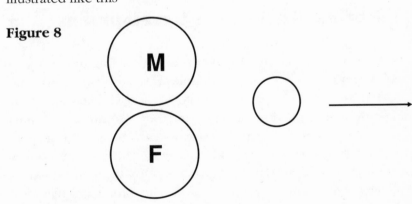

During the latency period, children learn to relate to adults other than their parents and to children other than their siblings. They begin to focus on relationships with children of the same sex and may ignore or move away from peer activities that include children of the opposite sex. Boys prefer boys and often don't like girls. Girls prefer girls and may avoid boys. Children develop very intimate "chum" or "best friend" relationships, and the behaviors that parents got used to during the individuation stage change completely. A boy will shrug and push his mother away if she tries to hold or kiss him. Two boys or two girls may walk down the street arm in arm. During this period, children explore and learn the ability to relate to people of the same sex and form both intimate and casual friendships with them.

The latency period also covers grades one through six. Massive knowledge must be learned and mastered, from reading, writing, and arithmetic to subject information and study skills. Children who did not resolve or master each stage of psychosocial development before entering this grade school age can have difficulty functioning in school or mastering the required tasks.

This period of consolidation ends by age 12 or 14. Adolescence arrives and, with it, new tasks to master. Everything is about to change, possibly for the worse, but eventually for the better. It is critical that each stage of child psychosocial development be mastered and that the child feel comfortable as he or she enters adolescence. If any previous developmental stage was not resolved, the child might have more difficulty with adolescence.

❖ Normal Adolescent Development ❖

Adolescence is a difficult time for almost anyone going through it, as well as for almost all parents. The period of adolescence prepares a person to move out of childhood and into adulthood. Because opportunities and world situations change and because society's values change, this transition has to be unique for each generation. Parents often rely on their own models and experiences, responding to their teenage children as their parents had responded to them or as they think their parents should have responded. The difficulty is that these role models and experiences more or less successfully prepared today's parents for the last third of the 20th century. Today's adolescents have to learn to live in the first part of the 21st century. As parents of adolescents, you will have to speculate right along with your teenage children on the strengths, attitudes, and skills that they will need for their adulthood. Your own life experiences will be out-of-date and probably too restrictive.

As parents, you must teach your adolescents the values that you believe are important, but you must also take into account the unique issues they struggle with in the world as it is now and as it will be for them. It is as if you have to give them roots and wings at the same time. They will need the roots—the security that comes with a solid foundation—in order to spread their wings and fly.

Adolescents must rework most of the psychosocial tasks of childhood. Physical growth still plays a major role in the stages of psychological growth. Some adolescents go through these stages with little or no difficulty; others have problems with a particular stage, but then regroup and move forward.

Problems With Physical Change

It is useful to distinguish between puberty, the period of physical changes, and adolescence, the period of psychosocial changes. Ideally, the two occur hand-in-hand; however, with some teenagers, these processes get way out of sync. When this happens, the adolescent has to cope with even more stress than usual.

Think of a girl who, at ten or eleven, is taller than all the other girls her age, full-breasted, and already menstruating, or the 17-year-old boy who is five feet tall, with peach fuzz and a high voice. Both are physically normal, but each is at a different end of the normal growth curve. And each has additional stresses to cope with. The reverse can be equally stressful. The boy in sixth grade who is already almost six feet tall and growing a beard or the short, flat-chested young woman who still looks like "a little girl" when she graduates from high school, each must cope with more than his or her share of the stress that adolescence normally brings.

Just as children do, adolescents have feelings and thoughts that cause conflicts and tension. However, adolescents' physical growth has also given them capacities for action and reaction that no child has. When a six-year-old boy cuddles with his mother, he feels pleasant sensations; when a 14- or 15-year-old boy does so, he may be embarrassed when he has an erection. A little girl can thoroughly enjoy sitting on her father's lap, but a 13-year-old girl who does so may have physical sensations that worry her. Wrestling with or tickling a sibling of the opposite sex can become both sexually stimulating and distressing. These new reactions that come with physical maturation may be so upsetting that the adolescent feels forced to transfer the relationships that cause these feelings to "safer" people outside of the family.

The same is true for angry feelings. It is one thing for a little boy to feel rage at his mother when his eyes are at the level of her knee caps. It is another situation when the angry adolescent realizes that he is taller and bigger than his mother and that he could really hurt her.

The distress and loss of confidence caused by these physical and emotional changes encourages the early adolescent to become more dependent on home and parents. However, the same newly discovered emotional feelings and physical reactions make it more difficult to explore and work out relationships and problems with parents and siblings. Thus there is conflict within the adolescent and eventually within the family. One pull is to become more dependent and child-like; the other pull is to become more independent and adultlike.

Initially, younger adolescents may attempt to cope with all this by using fantasy, choosing to relate to people who are unavailable and therefore safe. Boys and girls have "mad crushes" on movie stars, rock musicians, and sports heroes. The probability of a rock music star suddenly knocking on the door of an adolescent girl and asking her for a date is remote enough to allow her to safely fantasize a relationship with him. Gradually, however, young adolescents begin to explore relationships with real, potentially available people. At first, these interactions are likely to occur within groups, then within smaller groups, and finally with individual people. Very early dating is usually narcissistically motivated: adolescents want to date someone who makes them look good—the cheerleader, the football hero, someone whom everyone thinks is desirable. Often a boy behaves toward his date much as he would toward a boy friend, clowning around, showing off, or hitting. Later on, both adolescent girls and boys will date someone who makes them feel good. Looks are still important, but less important than personality.

Independence

The first task of adolescence is to move from being a dependent person to being an independent person. The initial struggles often revolve around the concepts of sex roles and identification. The old techniques that the child used to master separation may turn up again.

Negativism reappears: "No, I can do it myself" or "Don't tell me how long my hair can be" or "Don't tell me how short my skirt can be." This negativism is a renewed attempt to tell first you (the parent) and then the world that this growing person has a mind of his or her own. And again, it becomes an active verbal way of expressing anger. Adolescents seize on almost any issue to show that they have a mind separate from that of their parents. Parents and adolescents may argue about choice of friends and peer groups, school plans and courses, or points of philosophy and etiquette. Clothing and hair styles have always been favorite issues with which adolescents prove their independence. The casual or unisex theme of today resembles the "cause" of every other generation—the "flappers," the "zoot-suiters," the "rockers," the "hippies," and so on. Each generation recalls how they used clothes, hairstyles, and other external badges (earrings for boys; multiple earrings for girls), the more shocking the better, to show their parents they had a mind of their own.

All the old struggles over expressing love and anger reappear as new issues. What do you have to do to be loved? To keep love? To show love? What do you do with angry feelings? All of these questions have to be worked through with family and friends. In the process, adolescents begin to develop more consistent concepts of relationships and styles of expressing feelings. Their adult personality is beginning to form and emerge.

In the process of gaining independence, adolescents probably need to reject their parents' values and to reformulate their own value system. Unless this happens, their parents remain with them forever in the form of the conscience programmed in as a child. Teenagers need to rework these previously accepted values to fit with their todays and tomorrows. They will probably reject their former values at first, pointing out contradictions in their parents' values. They may feel that "no one over 30 can be trusted." They may challenge their parents for giving conflicting messages: "What do you mean, all people are created equal—you get mad at me if I date someone who's Jewish [or Protestant, or Catholic, or Black, White, Hispanic, or Asian]" or "Why should I be honest—you cheat on your income tax" or "Why shouldn't I drink [or smoke]—you do."

This interim "vacuum," when old values are rejected and new ones have not been established, can be upsetting. Some adolescents temporarily take refuge in "prepackaged" systems: organized religion, pacifism, the Boy Scout oath and laws, or some other value system or ritual. For others, their peer group provides this interim system. Closed cliques (the "in" groups) often set rules about all kinds of behavior—how to dress, who to talk to, who is "in," and who is "out."

Slowly, adolescents begin to blend many different values from all kinds of sources into their own existing values. By young adulthood, a new conscience, or superego, is established. The compatibility and flexibility of this new superego strengthens their ability to handle and express feelings and emotions in relationships. All through life this superego will have to be able to change and grow in order to accommodate new life situations.

As adolescents begin to feel independent of their family and as the family supports and encourages this emerging maturity, the question of the three to six year old is heard once again: "Who am I?" The answer, of course, can no longer be "just like Mommy [or Daddy]."

Identity

Thus the second developmental task of adolescence, establishing one's identity, begins. Becoming a "chip off the old block" is not enough and can be too restrictive. Unlike the child, the older adolescent will select characteristics from many people—religious leaders, teachers, neighbors, relatives, parents, friends, maybe even famous people—blending certain of their features with her or his own to become a unique new person. This new person, or identity, is not the adolescent's final self, but it forms the basis of what he or she will become. One's identity must be reworked throughout life as roles change; one must adjust to becoming a graduate, a spouse, a worker, a parent, a grandparent, and a retiree.

Each generation and each culture exert different social and cultural pressures on human beings. The child growing up in the Victorian era heard very different messages from the outside world than did one growing up in the "wild" decade of the post–World War Twenties. The adolescent growing up in the post-Vietnam world of the Eighties and Nineties experiences different social and cultural standards than her or his parents did. Let me note once again that it is crucial for parents to understand and accept that their adolescent lives in a different world than they did as adolescents and that their adulthood will be different as well.

The total developmental process that begins at birth culminates in an identity for each person. If your child successfully masters all of these tasks, he or she will have a successful functional identity with healthy and positive feelings about himself or herself. If any tasks are not successfully mastered, this identity can be restrictive or dysfunctional.

Intimacy

The adolescent has one remaining task to master. Until this time, relationships have been based primarily on a child-adult model. Now the adolescent or young adult has to learn to relate successfully to other people and eventually to one other person, as equals, on a one-to-one basis. This kind of relationship is often referred to as "intimacy." The task starts in late adolescence, but it is not complete until young adulthood.

When people relate in a dependent-independent mode, they need and depend on significant and more powerful people, like parents. When young, children may very well feel as if they and their parents are one. This is intimacy, but not a workable kind of intimacy in an adult world. In an adult intimate relationship, in the independent-independent mode, each person depends on the other. However, even though each loves, leans on, and needs the other for his or her emotional well-being, neither loses his or her boundaries. At all times, each can still function independently and well. This is a goal that most of us work on all our lives and few of us achieve with total success. But, because it represents the best that human beings can make of their adult relationships, it makes a fitting close for our discussion of normal development.

Chapter 6

Associated Emotional and Social Problems

As I began to prepare this chapter, I received a call from a parent ("Mrs. A"). She wanted me to see her nine-year-old son, "Bobby," who had just been suspended from the fourth grade because of fighting. Over the telephone, Mrs. A commented that Bobby had been a problem most of his life. Let me use Bobby's case as an example of the emotional and social problems often found with children who have attention-deficit hyperactivity disorder (ADHD).

❖ Case example ❖

I saw Mr. and Mrs. A alone first. Mrs. A said that there had been no problems with the pregnancy or delivery and that she had brought Bobby home from the hospital on the third day. She described the first three months he was home, however, as impossible. Bobby had colic, and feeding him was difficult. Their pediatrician had to try several milk formulas before finding a soy-based one that seemed to help. On top of this, Bobby did not sleep well. He would sleep for two hours and then wake up crying. He did not sleep through the night until he was ten months old. Mr. and Mrs. A recalled these months as a "living hell" because nothing seemed to comfort him.

Bobby's motor and language skills had developed at the age-appropriate times. Mr. A recalled that Bobby started to walk at ten months and that, "at ten months and one minute you had to chase him or he would run out of the house." His parents told me there were no other major problems until he was two years old, when they started toilet training him. This, they said, was difficult. Bobby was finally bowel trained by age two years, ten months. But at age nine, he still continued to wet his bed each night (the medical term for this is *enuresis*).

Mr. and Mrs. A enrolled Bobby in a part-time nursery school when he was three years old, but the staff suggested that he was not ready for school. They said he would constantly run all over the room, not pay attention to the group, and hit other children. Bobby's parents told me he was the same way at home. He was always on the move, he wouldn't sit in their lap and listen to a story, and he had a "short fuse" and would cry or hit if he couldn't get what he wanted or if his sister (two years older) made him unhappy.

When Bobby was four, his parents enrolled him in nursery school again. He had difficulty throughout the year. His teachers complained that he would not sit still during circle time or pay attention to the group activities. Often, he would get up and wander about the room. If another child did not do what he wanted he would hit the child.

Although kindergarten was no better, Mr. and Mrs. A said there was some improvement when Bobby was in the first grade. He had a firm but caring teacher who stayed on top of him. She also allowed him to walk about if he wanted. The next year, however, was not a good one. Bobby's second-grade teacher complained about his not staying in his seat and his constant fidgetiness. Each report card noted that he could do so much better if he would just stay on task and complete his work. Bobby would occasionally get into trouble with the other children during unstructured times like recess. Third grade was much the same.

Bobby started fourth grade promising his parents he would be a good boy this year, but by the end of October Mr. and Mrs. A had been called in for a conference. Bobby's teacher told them he was constantly moving about the room and bothering the other children. Even when he worked at his desk, he would distract the other children by tapping his pencil or playing with his books. The teacher thought him to be immature because he would not stay on task and complete his work unless she worked with him. The other children seemed not to like him and often teased him. She asked Mr. and Mrs. A to talk to Bobby and to get him to understand that he was now in fourth grade and had to grow up.

In late December Bobby hit a boy who was teasing him. This boy's mother called to complain, and Bobby was suspended from school for three days. The principal told Mr. and Mrs. A that they needed to get help for him before he "grew up to be a delinquent."

When I questioned them, Bobby's parents agreed that he had been active and fidgety his whole life. They, too, could see that he had a difficult time paying attention. Whether they were reading to him, he was playing with his toys, or he was doing homework, Bobby was constantly distracted to other activities. He had always had a short temper, striking out or having a tantrum if frustrated. In addition, they said that he stole money from them. Because he was their first boy, they had assumed that boys were just different from girls.

When I met Bobby, I found him to be a delightful, pleasant boy. During the evaluation sessions he was not active, and he did not appear to be distractible. His choice of play objects, play, interactions, and fantasy appeared to be appropriate for his age. After the second session with him, I wondered why my observations did not match the history given by his parents.

With his parents' permission, I spoke with Bobby's teachers and his scout leader. Each described his hyperactivity, distractibility, and impulsivity. I had to conclude that my office was quiet and had few distractions and that in my sessions Bobby had no academic demands and received one-to-one attention from me. The real-life descriptions by the others were more valid than my office observations in assessing him for hyperactivity, distractibility, or impulsivity.

At the time of the evaluation, Bobby was not functioning in school. He had poor peer relationships, and his behavior at home resulted in constant yelling, fighting, and punishment. Both his teachers and his parents were overwhelmed and felt helpless.

Bobby's problems are not unique. The common theme is a chronic and pervasive history of hyperactivity, distractibility, and impulsivity. An early history of difficulty with eating, sleeping, and irritability is not uncommon among children with ADHD. Year after year the teachers correctly identified the behaviors, but no one recognized the probable cause. Each projected his or her frustration and anger onto the child and the parents. By the time Bobby came to see me there were emotional, social, and family problems. However, these problems were secondary to an unrecognized and untreated disorder and were not the primary disorder. If individual and family psychological interventions were started, he might have improved for short periods of time but the hyperactivity, distractibility, and impulsivity would have persisted. By treating the ADHD in addition to providing the needed individual and family help, the total clinical picture could be improved.

ADHD is believed to be a neurologically based disorder. Bobby's case illustrates that, for many children, ADHD had probably been present since birth and that the behaviors were apparent from the earliest years. This case also illustrates that ADHD is not just a school disability; it is a life disability. The same behaviors of hyperactivity, distractibility, and/or impulsivity that interfere with school availability and performance also interfere with family life and with relating to other children. It is not uncommon for children and adolescents with ADHD to develop emotional, social, and family problems. In this chapter, I focus on the emotional and social problems. I will address family problems in Chapter 7.

❖ **Emotional and Behavioral Problems** ❖

Because of biases relating to how children and adolescents are referred for evaluation, many with ADHD are evaluated and diagnosed as being emotionally disturbed. Studies show that children and adolescents with ADHD who are hyperactive and/or impulsive are more likely to be identified as having a problem and more likely to be referred for evaluation. Children and adolescents with ADHD who may be only distractible are often missed. These individuals are frustrated and may have academic difficulties; however, they do not disrupt the class and, thus, do not get referred for evaluation. Girls who are only distractible appear to be the group of ADHD children and adolescents most often missed. For cultural reasons they are less likely than boys to show their frustration.

The hyperactivity, distractibility, and/or impulsivity of ADHD create stress with all aspects of psychological and social development.

How these behaviors impact on the psychosocial functioning of the child or adolescent with ADHD and how these behaviors are expressed are influenced by the individual's culture, age, and gender, as well as by the family, school, and community acceptance of such behaviors. Each child or adolescent will develop a specific set of resulting behaviors. Each might develop coping strategies or become dysfunctional.

Problems in the Early Stages of Development

Infancy may be very difficult for the child who will later be found to have ADHD. Some parents report possible evidence of ADHD occurring even before birth; for example, some mothers say that this child kicked more in the uterus than her other children did.

It is not uncommon for parents to observe that their child with ADHD was irritable and difficult to calm or comfort from birth. He or she never slept or only slept for brief periods of time. As an infant, he or she was colicky, and feeding was a chore. For some, these behaviors did not improve until about age three or four; for others, the behaviors remained as personality characteristics throughout childhood.

It is clear that these subtle, invisible, neurologically based problems have a significant impact on the earliest parent-child bonding and interactions. It is also clear that these problems can make parents feel insecure and inadequate. They try hard to comfort and please their infant but nothing works. They get little sleep and may become frustrated and irritable with the infant. Neither the infant nor the parents' emotional state encourages a warm and comfortable type of relationship or feelings of enjoyment.

Problems With Each Developmental Stage

Mastering separation.   For a child to learn to separate from his or her parents, two situations must occur. First, the child must feel secure enough to venture out and explore the world. Second, this world must be attractive and fun enough to make the child want to stay out there and engage with the people in it. The child with ADHD plus possible learning disabilities may have difficulty interacting with others, communicating, or doing what the other children are doing. He or she may find the outside world stressful and retreat or feel forced back to the inside world of home. Parents may sense this discomfort and lack of success and intuitively reach out to comfort. If there is hesitation to let go by parent and/or child, mastery of separation will be delayed.

As a result, children who do not master separation may prefer to stay at home. When things do not work out in day care or nursery school, they resist going. If forced to go, they avoid the other children or interact poorly with them. As these children struggle to master separation, their parents begin to see the negativism, the power struggles, the need to control, and the difficulties with relationships (that were normal for the two year old) persisting to age three, four, and beyond.

Mastering individuation. If a child is having difficulty with other children, with play activities, and with preschool situations, how can they successfully work out the question "Who am I?" These problems of the three to six year old may persist, and this child will appear to be less mature than his or her peers. Even after age six, this child may continue to be fearful and have nightmares, may try to split adults and other children, or may avoid certain activities for fear of being hurt. When these behaviors extend into kindergarten and the first grade, teachers become upset and classmates become angry.

Moving into latency. It is critical for children to enter the learning years (first grade and beyond) with a good sense of trust in adults, comfort with being away from their parents and family, and an awareness of who they are. If any of these earlier stages of development are not worked through successfully, the child at age six may enter latency and school with problems. They may be less available for learning, or their behaviors may make them unavailable for participating in the learning environment. If these earlier stages of development were only partially resolved, the child might do well initially but return to earlier behaviors under stress. If such problems appear and the child is seen by a mental health professional, it is critical that the ADHD plus possible learning disabilities be identified, as well as the impact each has had on the child. To only see the surface behaviors and diagnose the child as being emotionally disturbed without understanding the neurologically based problems that also exist will result in an unsuccessful treatment intervention.

Specific Emotional Problems

If a child is hyperactive, distractible, and/or impulsive and the diagnosis of ADHD is not recognized and treated, he or she will become increasingly frustrated and unsuccessful. Some children may handle their pain and frustration by externalizing their problems, some may internalize their problems, some may somatize their problems, and some may learn to influence their environment as a way of coping.

Children who externalize their problems are most apparent and, thus, most often recognized and evaluated. They appear to have a short fuse and quickly lose their temper. Hitting, fighting, and verbal attacks are not uncommon. At school, problems appear to be more likely to occur when they feel inadequate to the task or frustrated. At home, problems often relate to times when they are asked to do something they do not want to do or when they are not allowed to do something they want to do.

When children with ADHD internalize their problems, they feel the pain and anxiety. These children will develop a poor self-image and low self-esteem and are often sad or depressed, saying things like "I'm no good" or "I'm dumb" or "I'm bad." Often these feelings are confirmed by teachers and parents who, frustrated and not knowing why these children act the way they do, make comments such as "You are a bad boy" or "What you just did is bad" or "You keep this up and you will never learn anything."

Children who somatize their anxiety and frustration may have specific complaints, such as a headache or stomachache. Or bodily concerns might be less clear to them or might change; they might make comments like "I can't go to school today. My elbow is sore" or "I don't want to go out and play. My throat feels funny."

Perhaps the most successful way for these children to cope is by manipulating their environment. They learn what to do to the wrong person at the wrong time to disrupt the lesson plan or to be kicked out of class. They become the class clown. If successful, they can avoid specific class work or be removed from class. In addition, such behaviors might appear to win a certain amount of peer acceptance as the other children talk about their deeds.

Specific Behavioral Problems

For many children with ADHD, the clowning or acting-out behaviors seem to be enough. For others, these behaviors progress into an oppositional defiant disorder or a conduct disorder. As noted in Chapter 3, it is unclear why these disruptive disorders are seen so frequently among children who have ADHD. (See Chapter 3 for discussion of possible reasons.)

❖ Emotional and Behavioral Problems ❖ of the Adolescent

Adolescence can be stressful for anyone. The stress is much greater if the person has ADHD plus possibly a learning disability. If he or she receives the proper help, the stress might be less. If the problems are not recognized until adolescence, much psychological damage might have been done, making adolescence that much more difficult.

As discussed in Chapter 1, about 50% of children with ADHD continue to have the disorder into adolescence. If the family doctor has not kept up with the literature, still believes that these children "outgrow" their ADHD by puberty, and thus takes the adolescent off of medication, all of the ADHD behaviors may return and cause difficulties at school, with the family, with activities, and with friends.

Each stage of adolescent psychosocial development can be impacted on by the ADHD. These difficulties often frustrate the parents and the school staff. They certainly frustrate the adolescent.

Moving From Being Dependent to Being Independent

As when the child masters separation, there are two issues involved for the adolescent in moving from being dependent to being independent. First, he or she must feel confident enough to move out and explore their world. Second, he or she must find this world safe and welcoming. If either issue is a problem, all of the normal early adolescent behaviors seen during this stage of development may be magnified or may continue beyond the point when they should no longer be necessary.

An adolescent who is insecure, has a poor self-image, and does poorly with his or her peers may not be able to move away from his or her family comfortably. Instead, he or she may turn away from outside contacts into the home, appearing to be content and preferring to be alone at home or watching television.

If the feelings of being dependent are stressful, negativism, power struggles, and unacceptable clothing or hairstyles may become an issue. The need for control may lead to noncompliance with treatment. The adolescent who readily took his or her medication as a child may now rebel and refuse to cooperate and take the medicine. If the adolescent has a learning disability, he or she might now refuse to go to the special education program at school or to see the tutor after school.

The normal rebelling against rules and authority figures expands to include increased problems at home and in school. As a parent, you are often in a no-win situation. If you insist that your son or daughter act his or her age, your adolescent suddenly acts like a five year old. If you baby her or him, your adolescent erupts in anger, complaining that you are treating him or her like a child. If you back off and leave him or her alone, your adolescent accuses you of not caring. If you give him or her adultlike freedom or responsibilities, he or she abuses the privileges then gets angry when you take them away.

Establishing One's Identity

Once some beginning sense of independence has been achieved, the great task of adolescence becomes finding one's identity. This task is difficult at best in a world in which value systems change, career opportunities change, and options expand and diminish unpredictably. Establishing an identity is even more difficult when a person feels like a failure at school, in the family, and with peers.

Some adolescents remain immature and childlike in their behaviors. They appear to be bland and passive, showing no personality of their own. Or they might be unstable, changing their minds constantly and not knowing what or who they want to be. This phase of adolescence is a time when being different is less tolerated. It appears that adolescents have to be "just like" their peers to be accepted. Only later can individual differences be accepted. Adolescents with ADHD plus possible learning disabilities feel different and are often seen as different. Peer acceptance is a problem. Again, it might be easier to withdraw into the house and retreat from peer interactions.

Some adolescents may be so desperate for social acceptance that they become vulnerable to peer pressure and act inappropriately, getting into trouble. Some may move into alcohol or drug use because "their friends" do and they want to be accepted. Boys might try acting "tough," dressing and acting like a heavy metal rock star. Girls might become sexually active, trying to get acceptance in this way.

Beginning to Learn of Intimacy

The task of intimacy begins late in adolescence but is really worked on more in early adulthood. For the adolescent who has not comfortably handled the earlier stages of development, the opportunity for relationships is so limited that the learning of intimacy does not take place. Dating and close friends are not available.

Poor self-esteem and low self-confidence lead adolescents to not risk close relationships. Their previous reputation and current behaviors may not encourage others to reach out. The longer their limited successes or isolation exist, the greater their problems become.

❖ **Social Problems** ❖

Children and adolescents with ADHD often do not relate well to peers and may not be accepted by these peers. They may have problems with classmates and neighbors. Difficulties can be found in out-of-school activities such as scouts, organized sports, and religious education. This peer rejection can be devastating and can lead to feelings of loneliness, poor self-image, and low self-esteem. For adolescents, such problems and feelings can lead to poor school performance, juvenile delinquency, and dropping out of school. Research has shown that the longer-term outcome for children without positive peer relationships can include occupational difficulties, alcoholism, significant psychiatric disorders, and antisocial behaviors.

In addition, some children and adolescents feel so out of control that they will try to dominate their environment. When among their peers, they need to control what is done and how it is done. They can be bossy and demanding. For others, their frustration may result in anger. In impulsive children this anger can result in aggressive behaviors. Adolescents may annoy their friends with their constant activity or with their inability to pay attention.

Many adolescents with ADHD have difficulty with social skills and awareness of social cues. They do not recognize the tone of voice or the body language that suggests their behaviors are annoying someone. They may have limited age-appropriate social skills needed to interact in a positive way with peers. If they are impulsive, each of these problems is made worse. They not only do not read the social situation well, they often act or speak before they think, resulting in behaviors that annoy or anger peers and result in peer rejection.

All of these problems are seen in school: in the classroom, in the halls, and on the playground. Each of the behaviors causes difficulty. These students can be disruptive in the classroom. They may be inattentive and require frequent comments from the teacher to return to the task to be done. They may be verbally intrusive, interrupting the teacher or other students. Their increased activity level, calling out and making noises, increased contacts with classmates, and frequent fidgeting impact negatively on teachers and on the other students.

Students with ADHD often have academic difficulties. Each of the behaviors associated with this disorder can interfere with their success in school. Attentional difficulties may result in a problem sustaining attention and easy distractibility by any noise or activity in the classroom. Work may be incomplete or not finished on time. Impulsivity may result in rushing through work or putting down their first thought. This lack of reflectivity may result in frequent erasures and errors, careless mistakes, and incorrect work. The overall result may be performing below their abilities and possible failure. The combination of annoying behaviors in the classroom, frequent corrections by the teacher, and poor academic performance may lead the other students to view these children or adolescents as dumb, thus contributing to peer rejection.

❖ **Summary** ❖

If a child or adolescent is diagnosed as having ADHD, the associated emotional and social problems must be recognized and identified. The treatment plan must address these problems as well as the ADHD. Such treatment approaches are discussed in later chapters.

The critical question for the clinician is whether these emotional and social problems are causing the hyperactivity, distractibility, and/or impulsivity or are a consequence of ADHD. Each conclusion leads to a different understanding and a different treatment plan.

Chapter 7

Family Reactions
to the Child or
Adolescent With ADHD

We have discussed at some length the problems that children and adolescents with attention-deficit hyperactivity disorder (ADHD) plus possible learning disabilities have in their relationships with people both outside and inside the home. The emotional and social problems of family members who not only want to, but have to deal productively with their daughters, sons, brothers, and sisters with these disabilities deserve special attention. I would like to start with a discussion of the normal reactions of parents and siblings, then go on to look at the larger problems that arise when perfectly normal feelings linger too long or become too extreme, thus becoming abnormal and possibly harmful.

When one member of a family suffers, everyone in the family feels the pain and reacts to it, sometimes with nearly equal distress. Parents, brothers, sisters, grandparents—all are part of this human system within which the child with ADHD lives and grows. Everyone in the family needs to understand the full range of problems the child has if anyone is to be of help. Everyone needs to understand her or his own reactions as well, and sometimes this is a painful and difficult process.

After your child or adolescent has been through an evaluation, someone on the evaluating team should explain the findings to you.

Your child too should know and understand, to the degree possible, what the findings are. Sometimes the evaluator takes care of this routinely. Rarely, however, does anyone (including the parents) explain the findings to sisters, brothers, and other family members. Yet it is imperative that everyone connected with the child know about and understand the problems.

As a parent, you undoubtedly had difficulty accepting that your son or daughter was different, that something was wrong. You may have experienced, or may yet experience, a series of reactions not too different from the grief reaction that people have when someone dear to them dies, although this grief is of lesser intensity. In a way, this reaction is valid. Initially, you might fear that you have to "give up" a part of your child or at least your ambitions for the child that you fear may never be realized. As we examine these reactions, don't become distressed. These feelings are not only normal, they are to be expected.

We shall go on to look at many of the problems that increase the stress the family already feels over the basic situation. If you recognize that any of these are serious problems in your family, you would do well to consult with your family physician or a mental health professional. Above all, don't feel ashamed to discuss feelings that may seem "selfish" or "unworthy" to you. These problems are real and your feelings are genuine. You must look at them squarely and deal with them. Keeping a stiff upper lip or denying that they exist only makes things worse for you and for your family.

I recently evaluated a ten-year-old boy who was a major behavioral problem in his family. When I met with his parents to review my impressions and recommendations, I started by saying, "You know, I hate to say this, but now that I have gotten to know your son, I must tell you that if he were my son I would have killed him by now." The boy's mother burst into tears. She was so relieved to hear that someone else could be as angry at this child as she felt.

❖   **Normal Parent Reactions**   ❖

As you know, in addition to being mothers and fathers, parents are also human beings. They have their own feelings and thoughts. They usually have mates with whom they enjoy intimate relationships, relationships that are often hard enough to manage successfully without additional family stresses. Having a child with a disability stirs up feelings, fears, and hopes that most people are unprepared for. These reactions affect the parents both as individuals and as a couple.

At no point is the stress greater than when the diagnosis is made—this is the moment when parents feel the first rush of anguish, fear, helplessness, anger, guilt, and shame, all at once. Nothing can describe the thoughts going through a parent's head as he or she rides home from the school or the doctor's office after the first conference. No sensitive professional should ever describe a child's problems to a parent without acknowledging these feelings and ending with a positive course of action such as "and this is what we will do about it."

Unfortunately, not all professionals are this sensitive. Some play what I call the "Ha, ha, you have leprosy" game. They throw out a lot of labels, banging a parent over the head with "Your child is disabled," and then say goodbye. Out the parents go, overwhelmed, with little understanding, hope, or direction to take with them. Or the physician says he or she wants to place your child on medication, but does not explain what ADHD is and why medication is indicated. He or she may not discuss how the medication works, what to look for, what the side effects are, or how safe it is. You are left with worries and perhaps with the fear that you are "drugging" your child.

Denial

As with other grief reactions, the initial phase of the grieflike reaction to the discovery of ADHD and possible learning disability is often *denial*: "It can't be true . . . the doctor must be mistaken" or "She only saw him for an hour; I don't believe it." You may doubt the competence of the bearer of such news and want to punish him or her. Frequently parents seek other opinions. Getting other evaluations can be useful. However, "doctor shopping" for one who will tell you what you want to hear does not do anything productive for your child.

Another form of denial is the "cover-up" reaction. One parent, usually the mother, wants to "protect" the other parent by not sharing the results of the studies or by minimizing the problems. Some parents successfully hide the fact from the other parent that their child is in a special academic or behavioral program at school. Sadly, the parent who is uninformed about the child's difficulties often continues to build up unrealistic expectations and demands results of the child that he or she cannot possibly produce. The child, seeing through this cover-up, perceives the true reason for it: "They can't accept me as I am; they have to pretend that I'm different than I really am." This often makes children quite understandably angry or sad, and they usually have difficulty accepting themselves when they do not feel that their parents can accept them.

After the Denial

Once a parent can "look" at the problems, he or she may feel over-whelmed with feelings of helplessness: "How could this have happened to me? Why me? What will we do?" Often, there is an effort to find an explanation for the helplessness. Somehow, if a reason can be found there might be some control over "it" happening again and the parent does not feel as helpless. It is not uncommon to wonder if the problems were caused by someone else, resulting in anger. The other possibility is that the parent is to blame, resulting in anger against one's self or in guilt. Let's look at these feelings and reactions.

Anger.   A period of anger commonly follows the denial stage. Parents may direct this anger inward, against themselves, or project it outward, blaming the other parent or any other outside source. On learning of a child's disability, it is normal to feel anger and other sentiments such as "Why me?" or "How could God do this to me?" or "How could I have done this?" or "How could *you* have done this?" or "We never should have had children!" This anger might be projected to people outside of the family. This reaction will be discussed later.

Guilt.   Parents may turn their initial anger inward, attacking themselves. They turn their anger against the self rather than against the problems. Often they feel depressed. Associated with this reaction may be feelings of guilt. It is a very short step from "How could I have done this?" to "It's all my fault." The parent may berate herself or himself with "God is punishing me because . . ." or "I didn't follow my doctor's advice" or "I've been given this extra burden to prove my worthiness." Some may feel guilty for the anger and punishment given this son or daughter before the reasons for the behaviors were understood.

As discussed above, for some people, feeling guilty and/or depressed represents an attempt to establish control over a situation that they perceive as basically hopeless and out of control. If a parent can lay the blame or attribute the cause to himself or herself, that person then "conquers" the situation by explaining it, however erroneously. The "logic" is that if this happened for a reason—on account of something one did—and if one does not practice that transgression again, then nothing like it will happen again.

Just as the child who feels depressed tends to become quiet and to pull away from people, so the depressed parent becomes isolated. If this depression is allowed to continue, the parent may withdraw from the child or the other parent at just the time that they (or other members of the family) need that person the most.

If initial anger has been displaced outward, the parent enters into a patter of blaming or attributing the fault to someone or something outside of herself or himself. Like the guilt reaction, blaming an outside agent at least places responsibility somewhere, and this too protects one from feelings of helplessness. The parent may blame the physician because "He didn't get to the hospital fast enough" or "I told her I was in labor, but she wouldn't believe me and I almost delivered in the car" or "If the pediatrician had come out to see him rather than prescribing over the phone, he wouldn't have had that high fever." A person may generalize this reaction to all professionals, who then become "bunglers," "incompetents," and "charlatans." Or a parent might say "It's the school's fault" or "She's just a young, inexperienced teacher" or "He's just a rigid old teacher." The teacher, doctor, or whoever is the butt of anger probably never hears these complaints. But the parent may never allow *the child* to forget them. Reactions such as these undermine the child's faith in and respect for the very people he or she must turn to for help and for hope.

Some parents attempt to suppress their guilt or their need to place blame somewhere else by overprotecting the child. The most normal, human thing to do when a youngster is hurting is to reach out and try to protect her or him. This is necessary and helpful. But a parent's goal must be to protect the child only where she or he needs protecting and to encourage the child to grow where she or he does not need protecting, even though that may be painful. A blanket of overprotection covers the child's weaknesses, but it also smothers the child's strengths. Not only does overprotectiveness keep a child immature and delay growth in areas where growth is possible, it also makes a child feel inadequate. He or she knows what's happening. When everyone else has a chore to do but your daughter does not, when everyone takes turns clearing the table but your son never has to, that child will very probably conclude, "See, they agree with me—I can't do anything." Such children may be poorly coordinated or unable to concentrate for any length of time, but they are as sensitive as you are, and maybe more so.

Most parents do work through these normal denial, anger, and guilt phases. When they do, they gradually become strong advocates for their children, mobilizing their energy in constructive ways.

❖ Pathological Parent Reactions ❖

Chronic Denial

Some parents cannot give up their denial. They continue to "doctor shop" in a continuing search for the doctor with the magic answer or magic cure or for someone who will say that nothing is wrong with their child. Such parents greet the newest professional on the block with flattery and praise, criticizing the many doctors, educators, psychologists, and psychiatrists whose opinions they have rejected. Ultimately, the new "hero" is also rejected and then attacked. As their frustration grows, they hop from one promised cure to another, often becoming the victims of those who capitalize on people in distress. This hopeless "shopping," of course, deprives the child of time that should be spent in constructive programs and the valuable therapy that he or she needs.

The chronic denial reaction has other potentially serious consequences. Because each "authority" fails, she or he must be downgraded when the parents move on to the next one. The child picks up the message not to have faith in anybody in any professional capacity. This faith and trust is absolutely necessary in order to have hope, and hope is absolutely necessary if one is to work toward overcoming the handicap. And, as I said before, the child also picks up that subtle but clear message: "We can't accept you as you are. We must find someone who will tell us that you are not the way you are." The child hears, knows, and reacts with anger, shame, and a conviction of inadequacy.

Chronic Anger

If parents do not resolve their initial anger and learn to handle it, they may continue to project it. Nothing can go right. Someone is always wrong in their minds: "After all this time and money, you haven't helped my child. How come?" or (to the child) "After all my efforts, why can't you learn anything?" Such parents, miserable themselves, are almost impossible for professionals to work with—or for their child to live with.

Chronic Guilt

When a parent handles his or her unresolved guilt by becoming overly dedicated to the child, that parent is apt to be covertly furious about it. What comes across in public is the dedication: "No task, no trip, no expense is too great to help my child." What comes across behind the scenes is the anger at having to do all of this and at having to give up things. Occasionally, a parent becomes a professional martyr. He or she never lets anyone forget how great the effort, how selfless the sacrifice has been. The surface behavior may be sweet and admirable, but somehow the child picks up the bitter parallel message: "Look how much I do for you, you ungrateful, good-for-nothing child. You're worthless to begin with, and you show no appreciation."

Parents may handle unresolved guilt by withdrawing from other social and/or family contacts and totally dedicating themselves to the child. Some parents carry this to the point where they have almost no energy left for relationships with the other children in the family or their husband or wife. Taking care of their child's needs becomes so demanding and taxing that they are too worn out, too weary, to meet the needs of the other children or for social activities or intimate relations with their spouse. The result is a dysfunctional family and, probably, a strained marriage. And, once again, often the anger at this state of affairs is not openly discussed between the parents but displaced onto the child who is seen as the cause of it all.

For other parents, the normal initial reaction of overprotecting the child might become a life-style, one that prevents growth for both the child and the parent and increases the child's feelings of worthlessness. Under these circumstances, the child can easily become infantilized. Occasionally overprotective behaviors may stem from a parent's attempt to cover up feelings of his or her own inadequacy as a person and a parent. People with low self-esteem and feelings of worthlessness may achieve feelings of being wanted and needed by deluding themselves that they are "all the child has in the world." When the child's existing immaturity and feelings of incompetence lead to failure, he or she naturally retreats back into the home. The overprotecting parent sees this and feels even more justified in moving in and protecting some more. A self-defeating cycle begins, the child increasingly realizing that she or he is helpless without the parent, and the parent reinforcing the notion that the child cannot survive without him or her.

Summary

It is expected that parents will experience the normal denial, anger, and guilt after they learn of their child's or adolescent's disabilities. It is not expected that these difficulties will continue and become a chronic pattern of functioning. If you see yourself or your spouse in these descriptions of more chronic behaviors, consider getting help so that the difficulties can be handled. This help will make you feel better and function better and will certainly help your child or adolescent.

❖ **Reactions of the Other Children in the Family** ❖

As discussed earlier, when parents suspect ADHD or a learning disability and become concerned, they usually take their child to one or more specialists. Finally someone explains to them what the problems are and what needs to be done about them. At some point, someone probably sits down with the parents and "interprets" the findings. Occasionally, but not often enough, someone sits down with the child or adolescent and explains to him or her what the problems are, what the events of treatment will be, and why. Almost never does anyone explain any of this to the child's brothers and sisters. Yet, they are part of the family, and they need to know. *When one member of a family hurts, everyone feels the pain and hurts.* When they are left in the dark, what are brothers and sisters supposed to do? How might they react?

The reactions of your other children may be made worse because you expect more of them than you expect of yourselves. The child or adolescent with ADHD and/or learning disabilities is very good at getting parents frustrated and angry. One parent may yell or hit; another parent might cry, withdraw, or pout. Your other children get just as frustrated or angry. Yet, if they yell or hit or cry or withdraw or pout they are often punished or told they may not act that way. They are human too. They are entitled to the same feelings you have. You cannot tell them not to have these feelings. They have as much difficulty controlling these feelings as you sometimes do. You cannot tell them not to role model their behaviors after their parents. You must acknowledge that they have normal and expected feelings and help them learn what to do with them. If they cannot act like their parents, teach them an acceptable way for expressing their feelings.

If the two parents disagree on parenting styles or discipline methods, the stress and conflicts between the other children and the child with the disabilities can cause major stress between the parents. This problem can be even worse if there the parents are divorced and the children spend time in two different families, each with a different style of responding.

Your other children and adolescents might struggle with many different feelings as they live with and try to cope with the child who has the problems. Let me review some of these reactions.

Anxiety

Some children become very worried and feel anxious. This is especially true in families where the cover-up is on and little, if anything, is said. "What's wrong with Jimmie?" they ask. Their parents answer, "Oh, nothing special . . . it's O.K." Yet they see the parents taking Jimmie from one place to another, and they hear phrases like "brain damage" or "Where are we going to get the money for all of this?" They see their sister or brother taking medicine but are not told why. They see mother or father upset, maybe in tears, maybe angry. Aware that something is wrong but not knowing what it is, their imagination may take over. Frequently they fantasize that things are worse than they really are, and then they worry. I have heard siblings say, "Is he going to die?" or "Will it happen to me?" or "If it's not important, why all the whispers and hush-hush?" Your other children must have clear information and all of the facts that they need to understand.

Anger

Sisters and brothers may become angry, fighting with the child who has the problems or with their parents. If double standards are in effect, you can be sure they will notice them and become angry: "How come I've got to make my bed and she doesn't?" or "He broke my toy and you didn't do anything" or "Why is it that when I do something I get punished and when he does the same thing I am told that I have to be more understanding?" Or the amount of time and energy the parents spend with the child who has the disabilities may make the other children very jealous. Taking the one kid to special tutoring, special programs, and doctors leaves little time or energy available for the others. This child demands most of the time spent on homework, leaving little time to help the others. So much money may be spent on this child or adolescent that everyone else has to do without or vacations have to be compromised. You can't really blame the siblings for complaining.

Furthermore, these children will undoubtedly have to take some teasing at school. "Hey, how's your spastic brother?" or "Your sister sure acts funny . . . she's so gross . . . is she a mental case?" Anyone, and especially a child, is embarrassed by such comments and gets angry. Even at home, the other children may not feel safe. Their parents insist that they let the sibling with disabilities, who has no friends, play with their friends when they come over and this sibling acts foolish, embarrassing them. Your other children may stop bringing their friends home for fear of what their brother or sister will do. Some will do everything possible to be at a friend's house as much as they can.

Guilt

Sisters and brothers may feel guilty too, and they may feel particularly guilty about their anger when the verbal or nonverbal message from their parents is "He can't help it" or "It's not her fault." This is a hard message to swallow for someone who has not yet gained a lot of perspective on life. Or a brother or sister may secretly think, "I'm glad it's not me," then feel guilt and/or shame for thinking such thoughts.

Acting Out

Because of these feelings of anger or guilt, a brother or sister might "act out" against their sibling with the disabilities. They may tease and provoke the child to encourage misbehavior, or they may do something themselves and then set up the child as a scapegoat. Because they are so frustrated and angry and they are told that they cannot show their feelings, they get even in these ways. As the parents punish the child with the problems, the siblings feel revenged. Sometimes siblings set up the child with disabilities to look or act bad simply because they think that the worse their sister or brother looks, the better they will look.

Covering up Success

A sibling without disabilities can also affect the child with disabilities negatively. It seems to be the plight of children with handicaps that a younger brother or sister is not only supernormal and delightful but precocious, quickly passing him or her academically and socially. This hurts. Yet, in all fairness to the other children, they must be encouraged to live up to their potential. They deserve encouragement and praise. Do not hold back or minimize praise for fear of hurting your son or daughter who has ADHD and/or learning disabilities. They have to learn to cope with reality.

Summary

There is no way that you can prevent some or all of these feelings from surfacing in your family. None of your children were born as self-denying, altruistic models of charity. Besides, all of these feelings, provided they are kept within limits, are normal and can be handled. The more you are aware of your behavior and the more you try not to have double standards or expect more from your children than they are capable of doing, the less there will be difficulties. The only way to forestall the worst of this anger among your children is first give them all of the facts, then let them know that it is safe and acceptable to discuss with you what they are thinking and feeling, and, finally, answer their questions rationally and honestly.

None of this will be easy, but you are their parents too. Later, in Chapter 12, I will suggest ways of handling unacceptable behaviors within the family. If you see that you need help in explaining your situation or if you feel that the family is not functioning well, don't hesitate to ask someone for help. Join a support group in your area. Let other parents help you help yourself and your family.

❖ Example of Normal Family Reactions: ❖ Danny

I first saw "Danny" for an evaluation when he was three years old. I followed his progress and worked with his family off and on for the next ten years. I still keep in touch with his parents. Shortly after the first evaluation, Danny's mother ("Mrs. B") began to keep a diary. Initially she tried to reconstruct her experiences with Danny from the time of his birth. I have interwoven Danny's clinical picture with excerpts from that diary. Mrs. B writes exceptionally well, often eloquently, but don't mistake this for a fictional account. As she confronts and finally begins to bring the various stages of her despair under control, you will be struck by the truth and validity of her account. Perhaps you will share her tears and pain because you have been there too.

Pregnancy

Mrs. B's third pregnancy, after two sons, one four years old, the other two, went without complication. Her comments reflect the anticipation with which both parents greeted this child:

> A third son? What a joy, what a delight, such pride for the Father—what pleasure for the only woman—the queen in a household of adoring men. The other two are dark-haired and dark-eyed like Mom and Dad. The third is a unique one with his blue eyes and strawberry blond hair. Grandma says he was meant to be a girl. Everyone agrees, "Well, if you had to have a third son, at least he's different." We didn't realize at that time just how different he was.
>
> Danny had the advantage of being the third child. By the time a third is born all of the anxieties implicit in the care and handling of a normal infant have vanished. No more fits of panic when the baby cries unexpectedly. No more wringing of hands at the first sign of a sniffle or loose bowel movement . . . just a placid, cool, nonchalant parent juggling baby on one arm, holding middle brother with the right hand, pulling the wagon laden with sand box toys with the other, calling to the oldest son to look both ways while crossing the street on his bike. The combination of self-confident Mother and animated, stimulating surroundings are calculated to make this third baby so happy, so comfortable, with none of the pressures or tensions that the other two had to endure. "They bring themselves up, these third children do. He'll be your easiest," our pediatrician assured us.

Delivery and the First Year of Life

Danny's delivery was normal, with no reported difficulties, as was his physical examination prior to discharge from the hospital. Mrs. B quickly noticed, however, that he was different from her other sons—irritable, overactive, and unable to focus. Feeding him was a problem and was often accompanied by his vomiting. The pediatrician treated him for colic. Danny also had trouble getting to sleep, and he often slept only three to four hours at a time. Sometimes he cried and thrashed about for 30 minutes to an hour. Holding him did nothing to comfort him. Several other early suggestions of neurological difficulties were present. Danny's skin was overly sensitive to touch, and he persisted with a tonic-neck reflex beyond the early weeks of life (that is, when his head was turned to the side, the arm on the side he faced pulled up).

Mrs. B felt that from the start Danny didn't like her. When she picked him up, he cried; the more she cuddled him the more he cried (the tactile sensitivity). When she turned his head toward her nipple, he pushed her away (the tonic-neck reflex). She felt helpless, inadequate, angry, and guilty. She did not yet understand, so she blamed herself:

> Well then, why did he cry so much? Why did he squirm in your arms as if pleading to be released to the security of his crib? Why the endless bouts of vomiting, before, after, during his meals? Why not the same show of pleasure at being rocked and played with like his brothers? Why no "coos" or "goos" or babbles or giggles? Where was this joyous, relaxed, happy third baby syndrome?
>
> By the end of Danny's first year of life, I attempted to review all of these statements regarding the easy routine with third baby—the enjoyment I was supposed to be savoring through him—the idea that "he's your last so lap it up" sort of notion. All I could come up with was a dull ache in the pit of my stomach. Why isn't he fun for me? Why doesn't he return my love? Why no give-and-take between baby and anyone? His constant crying and whining, his discontent and apparent discomfort, convinced me that he must be in some physical distress. That question, along with his persistent vomiting, brought me to the pediatrician who assured me that he was fine. I must relax and learn to loosen up. That along with a little sympathetic support was supposed to reassure me.
>
> But the dull ache in head, heart, and stomach persisted. Why the relief for me at Danny's bedtime? Why the feeling of incompleteness when he was around and the feeling of solidarity and wholeness without him?
>
> My growing conclusion was that there must be something wrong with me to result in this personality conflict. I was perplexed by my feelings of guilt in relation to this child, because if that were my pattern, why wasn't I feeling guilty in relation to my other children? I realized later that my guilt originated from ambivalent feelings toward him—feelings of love and hate, of sympathy and anger, of concern and fear. The insecurity that my relationship to him created

inside of me resulted in feelings of self-doubt about my capacity as Mother and in regard to my own emotional stability, which had never been in question.

My loneliness while submerged in these feelings was intense. In spite of a good marriage and a loving husband, I was alone. Many of these feelings and observations were not shared by my husband who wasn't with Danny as much as I, who never saw him vis-à-vis his age peers, and who by virtue of a very placid, calm nature had a greater capacity to accept a wide diversity of behaviors. Every attempt I made to acquaint him with my concerns was met with assurance that Danny was fine—perhaps a little immature, but fine. The family reminded me that I was older when I had him—perhaps two kids had been enough, all of this being after the fact. All I was left with were doubts, fear, and anger directed toward myself and toward this creature who was the source of all my problems.

By age three, Danny was diagnosed as having ADHD, learning disabilities, and sensory integrate disorder. In looking back over Danny's first year of life, as well as the lives of others like him, it is difficult to fully understand the impact these disabilities might have had. Danny was later diagnosed as having auditory perception disabilities. What effect did these disabilities have on his orienting to sound or on his learning to relate to or attach to his mother? What effect did his auditory figure-ground disability have? Could Danny orient at all to his mother's voice? How must he have perceived the world when being held was experienced as uncomfortable or painful? Mrs. B described her frustrations, confusions, and ambivalent feelings toward the developing relationship with her infant son. Could Danny's feelings have been any less troubled?

Years One and Two

Danny's language development was delayed. On top of everything else, he now became frustrated by his inability to communicate his needs. His gross motor development was also delayed, resulting in very slow mastery of sitting, standing, walking, and running. He was hyperactive and distractible. He did not outgrow his tactile sensitivity and became defensive to touch, avoiding too much body contact. Possibly because of these neurological problems, he had trouble dealing

with separation. His parents found handling him overwhelmingly difficult. With no information and no reassurance from her pediatrician,
Mrs. B continued to search within herself for an explanation:

By 13 months of age a lock on his bedroom door was required to
keep Danny protected from his own enormous fund of aimless energy, which was consistently directed toward destructive pursuits.
Perhaps his resentment at being locked in or an increasing hyperactivity was the cause of the extreme havoc he wreaked on his sur-
roundings. Linoleum was lifted up off the floor of his room. Pictures
in their frames were torn down from the walls, window shades were
replaced because they were ripped up. A rocking chair was used to
bang against the wall, thus creating dents in the plasterboard. A har-
ness held him down in his high chair and one was used in the stroller
when he was wheeled away from his exhausted Mother by an
equally reluctant baby-sitter. And all the time I'm thinking what is
wrong with me that I have created this child who I wish I never had.

The more I disliked him, the more he clung to me, the less able he
was to let me go, thus causing horrendous scenes at my departures,
serving to increase my guilt and self-blame. "When I leave he gets so
scared. Therefore, I shouldn't leave. But, if I don't I'll go mad. So, I'll
leave but he'll scream and I'll feel so awful." This internal dialogue
characterized every separation we were ever to endure.

His constant aimless running resulted in many falls and bruises,
the worst of which was a collision with Danny's nose and the dining
room table. Sutures were required for that accident, which was followed by several other close calls, all a result of his hyperactivity and
poor coordination. Along with this went the assaults by Danny upon
anyone who dared to get physically close. Once he was seated on my
lap, I would in a five-minute period of time receive several blows to
my jaw from the unpredictable banging of his head. His frantic
squirming discouraged me from holding him or cuddling him. Kicks
on my knees and in my stomach, little hands pushing my face away
from his—so many efforts to keep me away—all added up to one
conclusion: he doesn't love me and I don't love him and it's my fault
and it's unnatural and wrong and I wish I didn't have him and I've
ruined my life forever. And yet, there he sat with his sad blue eyes
and his confused forlornness. He was as unhappy as I was, and I had
to find out why.

Year Three

Danny's gross motor problems persisted. He began to develop language, but he often appeared to misunderstand or to respond in ways that made little sense. His parents felt that his thinking was more concrete than his brothers' had been at the same age. He developed fears of unknown places and of new objects. His separation problems persisted. Although toilet trained for bowel functioning by age two-and-a-half, he wet the bed at night (nocturnal enuresis). Mrs. B made the following entry in her diary when Danny started nursery school:

> At last Danny was three. A new era was ushered in by his enrollment in a nursery school—relief for Mommy and some friends (please God, some playmates) for Danny. But more importantly, at last some objective feedback from emotionally uninvolved teachers who see normal three-year-old kids all the time. No more would I have to rely upon Dad's calm assurances, upon Grandmother's accusations, upon my own frantic self-inquiry.
>
> Several months passed before the teachers decided that it was time to confront me with reality. Danny was not involved with the other children, they reported. Furthermore, he was tense, frightened, highly distractible, and most of all, very unhappy. It was with mixed feelings that I received this news. On the one hand I was very upset to hear my worst suspicions confirmed. On the other hand I was relieved to hear that someone else saw the same thing—that my sanity and clear vision need not be held in doubt any longer. Most of all, I was grateful for the sense of purpose and motivation that this shared awareness endowed me with.

It was at this point that Mr. and Mrs. B brought Danny in for consultation. In the course of the evaluation, his pediatrician, a pediatric neurologist, a special education professional, and a speech and language therapist saw him. I did the child psychiatric and the family evaluations. The concluding diagnoses included

1. Specific learning disabilities: auditory perception, sequencing, abstraction, auditory memory, difficulties with gross motor skills, and demand language disabilities
2. Hyperkinetic reaction of childhood (the term in use then for what

would now be ADHD), manifested by hyperactivity, distractibility, and impulsivity

3. Sensory integrative disorder, manifested by tactile sensitivity, defensiveness, and his motor problems
4. Emotional problems: separation anxiety, fears, and poor peer relationships
5. Family problems: overwhelmed, frustrated, helpless feelings by parents

Also noted was his inability, at times, to leave one activity and move on to another (called *perseveration*). The bed-wetting was seen as another reflection of a dysfunctional nervous system.

The following treatment plan was recommended and implemented:

1. Special education and language therapy in a therapeutic nursery school for children with learning and language disabilities
2. A trial on medication to minimize the hyperactivity and distractibility
3. Preventive family counseling focused on educating the parents about their child's disabilities and their role in helping

The medication, methylphenidate (Ritalin), significantly decreased the hyperactivity and distractibility. It also stopped the bed-wetting. (I have seen this effect of Ritalin with many children and wonder if the bed-wetting might be a reflection of the impulsivity. Perhaps, once the impulsivity is treated, the bed-wetting stops.) Mr. and Mrs. B learned to use deep touch stimulation when holding Danny, lessening his tactile sensitivity and, thus, his tactile defensiveness. He adapted to the new therapeutic nursery and slowly his language improved. The long process of special education therapy began.

Mrs. B described the evaluation and its impact. Her awareness of her feelings and the shift in her ways of handling them reflect the counseling:

It was these feelings that enabled me to have Danny evaluated. He was seen by many specialists, each seeming to focus on one part of his problem. By the end, all the parts came together and presto—a diagnosis—something to grab hold of, something to explain it all, and most of all a means, a method, a way to help.

Danny's neurological impairment caused perceptual problems which resulted in learning difficulties, we were told. His restlessness, his dislike for being touched and touching, his chronic unhappiness and frustration all could be explained by this syndrome. The cause of it was unknown. So who could be blamed? There was a way to help him . . . please tell us how. There is a way to handle him at home that will make him feel good and happy and worthwhile . . . please tell me and I'll try. It will take time but he'll get better . . . or will he??? How great!

So, with all this, I gazed upon my neurologically impaired Danny, lifted my eyes to the heavens and whispered, "Thank you. It's not as serious as I thought. Thank you. There is help available. Thank you. He will in time get better. Thank you, again. You are not a crazy, unlovable, unnatural Mother. Thank you; thank you; thank you!"

But if that's the case, why didn't anyone believe or support me? Why was I kept in this state of anxiety and fear all these years? Where were the experts or even the loved ones? Why didn't they trust me? Why didn't they hear? And so once again I was angry—a state that was becoming second nature to me—descriptive of my mood and personality.

The anger directed itself inward then because it was futile and un-economical to express it; I became sad, depressed, forlorn. In short, I felt pity for myself. Why did it have to happen to me? What did I do to deserve this? How will I ever find the strength to endure? How can I be a Mother to this poor, defenseless child? Days of brooding were to follow. I was caught up in a grief reaction that was all-consuming. I accused everyone of being unable to understand what I was going through. In a way I was trying to say, "Look how I am hurting. Won't someone take care of me and see how much I am caring?" The only problem with this behavior, I soon determined for myself, was that it accomplished nothing positive nor worthwhile and, furthermore, it led me to feel unattractive and selfish.

As soon as this awareness surfaced, a new era dawned. Self-indulgence, once completed, paved the way for the realization that Danny and I were going to be involved with one another for many years to come and that I'd better come to terms with his problem and begin to work on it with him so that both of us could be happier than we were. Thus I allowed myself to become informed by the professionals, comprehending the "whys" and learning the "how-tos." With this knowledge came understanding and with this understanding came coping and with this coping came a growing sensitivity toward his positive changes and progress. This encouraged me to continue with renewed courage and with expectations for Danny, based on the reality of the situation.

No longer was there room in my rationale for unproductive self-pity, brooding, or accusations. I realized that the effects of this attitude would result in more problems. Let's then acknowledge that we have a problem. Let's not be afraid to label it, to explore it, to learn about it, to deal with it, and to accept it.

Years Three Through Twelve

Although Danny remained in special education programs through the fifth grade, by the fourth grade he was in a regular education program, receiving special education and language therapy one hour a week each. He remained on Ritalin. His parents worked closely with his school programs and his teachers over the years. They carefully selected those peer activities and sports that tended to build on his strengths rather than to magnify his weaknesses. Each year brought successes and new challenges. Mrs. B reflected on these experiences:

> But, does acceptance defend a Mother against uncomfortable feelings? Does she ever adjust to the situation and simply continue her day-to-day existence, giving minimal thought or worry to this part of her life? The answer for this Mother is a resounding NO!
>
> The process of adjustment is an ongoing one. On his bad days I feel bad. Back creeps the old sense of fear and foreboding. On good days I feel hopeful and perhaps a trifle excited at the glimpse of health and wholeness I see under the surface. On most days I feel the responsibility of another day. I decided that I will try to begin at his beginnings—to love him, to accept him right where he's at. I realize I must plan according to his needs at that moment and with this comes the task of ignoring some of my own. No one can do that without feeling some anger.
>
> And what about the feelings of deprivation when you see how

poorly he measures up to his age group, and, as he grows older, how poorly he stands in relation to children even younger than he? What of the feelings you get when you see him rejected by children and adults alike because he can't relate in the expected, conformist manner? What of the embarrassment you feel when his problems result in antisocial behavior in public? What kind of excuses do you force yourself to fabricate to ease your self-consciousness? What do you say to family when they assure you that all he needs is some discipline and he'll fall into line? The disruption he causes in the tempo of family life—the interference with certain pleasures arouses anger, deprivation, and guilt. And how about the emptiness in your gut when you catch a glimpse of his inner world of confusion and of loneliness? How does that make you feel?

With all of these feelings resurfacing with every new situation, how can one ever expect to be adjusted? The only answer I have found is to make room for the feelings, to accept them—not to luxuriate in them, but not to deny them . . . to say them out loud to yourself or to whoever is unafraid to hear them. This paves the way for a stronger, more positive relationship with Danny.

The way I relate to Danny becomes reflected in the way he sees himself. If I allow his problems to scare me, he too becomes scared. Communicating to him that he is worthwhile and lovable and that I have hopes for him enables him to face his future with hope and courage. This places a great responsibility on me, but it is the only chance any of us have for a good life. If we have hope for Danny, he will have hope for himself.

I still wish I had three perfect sons. I occasionally indulge in that "wouldn't it be lovely" fantasy. I have come to treasure in the other two what many people take for granted. I have a great investment in them but I do in Danny too. It is an investment imbued by the implicit faith I have encouraged myself to have in him and in me. It will take a long time and it will be difficult, but I have hope that it will work.

Current Progress Note

I discussed this story in the first edition of my book *The Misunderstood Child* (see Appendix A). Danny was in the eighth grade then. Academically he was doing well. His peer relationships were limited and best handled one at a time. He related well to his parents and brothers but was described as "a little aloof" with others. He continued to need the medication. His psychological functioning was appropriate for his age.

As I prepared this book, I called Mrs. B. Danny was about to enter his senior year at an excellent college. Academically he was doing very well and had a B-plus average. He had learned to be very organized and efficient. His major was music. Mrs. B reflected that music had always been his "salvation." He was good and could escape into playing for hours at a time. At this time he plays the keyboard, composes, and records his music. He is well respected as a musician.

Danny still has social difficulties. He has friends, but no special friend. He has girls who are friends, but he has never had a girlfriend. He still does not have a good sense of humor, and, although much improved, he does not pick up many social cues well. Yet, he has completed three years of college and appears to be comfortable with himself.

Mrs. B ended our conversation by saying, "He's a real sweetheart, a lovely person. Yet, he is never going to be perfect . . . I hope he will not be a lonely person." Although she agreed that Danny had accomplished far more than any of us dared to wish for when he was three, four, or five, the worry about the future never ends.

Causes

Chapter 8

Causes of ADHD

A ny discussion on the cause (or *etiology,* as it is called in the medical literature) of attention-deficit hyperactivity disorder (ADHD)
must be considered as reflective of our current state of knowledge. It is
difficult to use much of the previous research information and some of
the current research studies because there is a lack of an agreed definition for this disorder. Many previous studies were done before the for-
mulation of the diagnostic guidelines found in DSM-III-R. Some earlier
studies examined hyperactivity only because it was the primary behavior noted in the earlier editions of DSM. Other earlier studies used the
criteria for minimal brain dysfunction and combined learning problems, hyperactivity, distractibility, and behavioral problems.

Another reason it has been difficult to review the previous research
findings relating to ADHD is that there are many factors related to attention. Recent research has supported this view. Thus there are a
group of attentional disorders of which ADHD may be but one clinical
type. This concern is discussed in more detail later in this chapter.

The current view is that ADHD is a brain-based or neurological disorder. How behaviors are manifested is influenced by both psychological and social factors. It is the interaction of both influences that
explain the life-picture seen with each individual.

For example, the way a child or adolescent expresses the frustration caused by ADHD will be influenced by culture and gender. A girl
with distractibility who is doing poorly in school and feeling frustrated
might withdraw and appear disinterested or depressed. A boy with the

same problems might misbehave and get into trouble. Each has ADHD, but the boy is more likely than the girl to be recognized and diagnosed.

Among the biological factors, the apparent genetic influence is important. Some studies suggest that 30% to 40% of children and adolescents with ADHD have inherited a familial pattern. Most likely, a parent, sibling, or other biological relative also has or had ADHD. This suggestive evidence of a genetic influence supports the brain-chemical theories on the cause of this disorder. Other studies have focused on other factors that might influence development during pregnancy.

These genetic, chemical, and other factors are discussed below. Because the rationale for the current treatment of ADHD with specific medications is based on a brain-chemical theory, this research area is discussed in more detail.

❖   **Genetic Factors**   ❖

Family studies, twin studies, and adoptee or foster home studies suggest an important genetic contribution to ADHD. Family studies show an increased risk of ADHD in children of parents who have nieces and nephews who have been diagnosed as having ADHD. Family studies also show increased risk in the siblings of boys diagnosed as having the disorder. Twin studies suggest a higher frequency rate for ADHD among identical (monozygotic) twins as compared with fraternal (dizygotic) twins. Foster children studies suggest an increased rate of ADHD among the biological parents of ADHD children compared with the rate found either among the parents of control subjects (children without ADHD) or among the adoptive, nonbiological parents of ADHD children adopted at an early age.

Another interesting observation is that the incidence of ADHD among children and adolescents who are adopted in the United States is about five time higher than would be expected among the general population. One could speculate about the parents of children placed for adoption or about the possible risk factors experienced during pregnancy and delivery; however, the reasons for such a high incidence are not known.

❖ **Neurochemical Factors** ❖

Before reviewing this area of research, I need to introduce you to certain terms. Messages are transmitted in the brain from one nerve ending to another by specific chemicals. These nerves are called *neurons,* and the chemicals are called *neurotransmitters.* There are about 50 known neurotransmitters. It is suspected that there are many more that we have not identified.

The neurotransmitters that have received the most attention in this area of research are called *catecholamine;* the specific catecholamine considered with ADHD is *norepinephrine.* Research suggests that ADHD is caused by a deficiency of norepinephrine in the brain stem area (specifically, the reticular activating system).

The research on norepinephrine that supports this neurotransmitter theory for the cause of ADHD comes from two sets of findings. One suggestive line of evidence relates to the observation that stimulant medications produce a significant decrease in the hyperactivity, distractibility, and impulsivity found with ADHD. Other evidence shows that these stimulant medications affect the brain processes involved in producing norepinephrine; that is, stimulant medications increase the production of norepinephrine in specific areas of the brain. These clinical and research observations that stimulant medications decrease the behaviors associated with ADHD and also increase the production of norepinephrine support the neurochemical theory that ADHD is a result of a deficiency of norepinephrine.

The second line of evidence suggesting that individuals with ADHD have a deficiency of norepinephrine in the brain stem area comes from research on the products and related chemicals produced when this neurotransmitter is broken down. These chemicals have been identified and measured in the blood, urine, and cerebrospinal fluid of children with ADHD before and after the use of these medications. Measurements of these chemicals show a decreased amount in individuals with ADHD before and an increase in these chemicals after the use of a stimulant medication. Thus the findings strongly support the theory that ADHD is caused by a deficiency of norepinephrine and that the stimulant medications decrease these behaviors by producing an increase in this neurotransmitter to the normal level.

❖ Research in Fetal Development ❖

Again, I need to review the terms used in this area of research. The term *natal* refers to the time of delivery. Thus the *prenatal* time is the time of pregnancy; the *perinatal* time is around the time of delivery; and the *postnatal* time is the time after delivery. Different chemicals circulate through the fetus during pregnancy. If these chemicals are natural to the mother (for example, glucose), they are called *metabolites*. If the chemicals are foreign to the mother (for example, alcohol or lead), they are called *toxins*.

Prenatal, natal, perinatal, and socioenvironmental factors may impact on the developing fetus. Examples of these factors might include poor nutrition, absence of prenatal care, an increase in metabolic or toxic factors, infections, or stress. Each can result in prenatal difficulties, premature delivery, and/or low birth weight. Studies have shown a relationship between low birth weight and prematurity and hyperactivity, distractibility, and aggressive behaviors.

There are two major long-term studies relating to child development currently under way, one in the United States and one in England. Researchers in each of these studies identified a large number of families at the time the mother first learned that she was pregnant. Each child has been studied extensively and will be followed into adulthood. It is hoped that the information collected might someday explain specific problems that a child might develop. In the large National Collaborative Perinatal Project in the United States, the evaluations done at age seven and ten found suggestive correlations between those children with hyperactivity, a short attention span, and impulsivity and the following prenatal factors: maternal cigarette smoking, convulsions during pregnancy, low fetal heart rate during the second stage of labor, lower placental weight, and more breech presentations (that is, born feet or legs first).

Other prenatal stresses have been examined in other studies. Infections, metabolic disorders, toxins, and diet deficiencies in the mother can result in children who show a higher incidence of ADHD behaviors, as well as evidence of a learning disability. The correlations in these studies are less strong than those in the National Collaborative Perinatal Project studies.

More recent studies of substance abuse during pregnancy are distressing. Many of these babies show problems with hyperactivity, distractibility, impulsivity, and irritability. Although these children might meet the criteria for ADHD, these behaviors should be seen as evidence of a more pervasive neurological disorder.

The above studies do not confirm cause and effect, but they do provide important evidence supporting a role for prenatal influences in the development of ADHD. Possibly, in some cases it is the genetic code and in other cases it is one or more of these prenatal factors or others not yet clarified that cause ADHD.

Postnatal Factors

Studies on trauma during delivery or in later life do not show a clear correlation with ADHD. There is an increased incidence of learning and behavioral disorders among children with seizure disorders, especially with epilepsy. However, it is not clear whether any specific behavioral disorders occur more frequently than others or if the behavioral disorder is associated with the epilepsy.

It appears that pervasive trauma to the nervous system can result in ADHD or ADHD-like behaviors. For example, one residual effect of viral encephalitis can be hyperactivity, distractibility, and/or impulsivity. Many children and adolescents who experience a closed head injury experience these same behaviors.

❖ Environmental and Cultural Factors ❖

Studies to date have not shown a relationship between ADHD and variables such as birth order, number of siblings, times moved, family income, mother's age, mother's educational level, or the father's educational level. The National Collaborative Perinatal Project did show suggestive evidence of environmental influences, although no correlation of cause and effect was noted: children with ADHD were more likely to come from homes where the father was absent. Perhaps the manifestations of ADHD are related to adverse social conditions, primarily disruptive family relationships, or perhaps ADHD behaviors contribute to causing disruptive families.

Cultural influences may play a role. Activity level, loudness, attentiveness, and inappropriate behavior are considered as normal and acceptable or not normal or acceptable by different cultures. Thus the same behaviors might be identified as a problem in some cultures and families and not in others.

❖ "Attentional Disorders" ❖

Some researchers express concern with the concept of ADHD as defined in DSM-III-R. They believe that there are other reasons for attentional problems that are not reflected by the clinical disorder of ADHD. Research on the broader concepts of attentional problems focuses on clarifying the process of attention in the brain and the multiple areas involved in this process.

One way of understanding this concept is to look at the issues involved in attention. It appears that there are at least three steps involved:

1. A person must find the appropriate stimulus and focus on it.
2. The person must sustain this focus.
3. When appropriate, the person must release this focus so that he or she can move to another stimulus.

Dr. Martha Denckla (of Johns Hopkins University in Baltimore, Maryland) has been attempting to expand the concept of ADHD by looking at the broad "executive functions" of the brain. She has noted that children with ADHD have areas of executive dysfunction, including difficulty with the planning and sequencing of complex behaviors, the ability to pay attention to several components at once, the capacity for grasping the gist of a complex situation, the resistance to distraction and interference, the inhibition of inappropriate response tendencies, and the ability to sustain behavioral output for relatively prolonged periods. Dr. Denckla has noted that these functions are heavily dependent on the integrity of the frontal lobes and their subcortical connections. In her studies, she has found that children with executive dysfunction have problems planning, organizing, and managing time and space. She believes that the academic failures that children with

ADHD have are explained by these executive dysfunctions. Her studies focus on four areas: 1) the ability to focus attention, 2) the ability to plan ahead and organize information, 3) the ability to shift and be flexible in processing information, and 4) the ability to inhibit extraneous or unnecessary responses. Perhaps ADHD relates to the first and/or the fourth of these areas.

Dr. Alan Mirsky (of the National Institute of Mental Health in Bethesda, Maryland) has been studying the process of attention in the brain and the specific areas of the brain involved with each function. His research is based on a neuropsychological model of attention that assumes that information processing occurs in sequential fashion. He and his colleagues see attention as a complex process or set of processes. They attempt to assign functional specialization of these components of attention to different brain regions, although they understand that some brain regions share more than one attentional function. Dr. Mirsky breaks attention down into a number of distinct functions: 1) the capacity to focus on or select some part of the environment, 2) the ability to sustain or maintain that focus for an appreciable period, and 3) the ability to shift adaptively from one aspect or element of the environment to another. Each behavior could be seen as part of the ADHD picture. Probably, the ability to sustain or maintain focus once selected is most relevant.

Dr. M. Posner (of the University of California, Los Angeles) has proposed a distributed neural system to account for the general properties of attention in human information processing. He and his colleagues have defined anterior and posterior attentional systems. The posterior attentional system is considered to be a "bottom-up" system, involved in the representation and processing of sensation. The anterior attentional system is considered to be a "top-down" system, involved in the representation and processing of action plans. Their research suggests that the posterior attentional system required to perform a visual orientation task is not dependent on a single area of the brain. Instead, attention in such a task may be dependent on several elementary attentional operations. They suggest three functions: 1) disengagement, 2) movement, and 3) engagement of attention. Their work suggests that the anterior attentional system may be related to the concept of sustained attention and thus to ADHD.

The research of Dr. James Swanson (of the University of California, Irvine) and others suggests that children with ADHD have no difficulty with the posterior attentional system; that is, they can shift from one focus or task to another. However, there may be an abnormal functioning of the anterior attentional system, resulting in a failure to sustain focused attention.

At this time, the research efforts on attentional disorders strongly suggest that the distractibility found in ADHD is secondary to an inability to sustain attention. Individuals with ADHD appear to be able to seek and then focus on the necessary task and then, when needed, shift focus to another task. However, they have difficulty sustaining attention while on task.

 ## Summary

Current research supports an interactive model for the cause of ADHD, incorporating both biological and psychosocial factors. A child's genetic endowment or other prenatal, perinatal, or postnatal factors might provide the biological basis for these behaviors. However, the clinical expression of these behaviors is influenced considerably by the child's culture and environment.

Current and future research might clarify that there are a group of attentional disorders and that ADHD is but one type of such disorders. Until further clarified, clinicians can only address ADHD as described in DSM-III-R.

Treatment

Chapter 9

Basic Concepts in the
Treatment of ADHD

The treatment of attention-deficit hyperactivity disorder (ADHD) must involve several approaches, including individual and family education, individual and family counseling, the use of appropriate behavioral management programs, and the use of appropriate medications. Each approach requires working closely with the school. In this chapter, I focus on the basic concepts in the treatment of ADHD. In the following chapters, I will address each aspect of this multimodal approach in turn.

Such a multimodal approach is needed because children and adolescents with ADHD have multiple areas of difficulty. To help your daughter or son, you must understand how the ADHD impacts on her or him in every aspect of life.

As discussed throughout this book, children and adolescents with ADHD often have a cluster of clinical difficulties. They may have a learning disability, some may have Tourette syndrome, and many develop secondary emotional, social, and family problems. It is ideal for the child or adolescent to be evaluated by a multidisciplinary team that can assess the total individual and can identify the areas of difficulty. If this is not possible, it is important that the person you select to be your primary clinician coordinate with the efforts of other professionals and with the school system when evaluating for each disorder. In some cases this clinician might speak to each professional involved in evaluating the child or adolescent then try to summarize the full findings. In other situations, this clinician will receive copies of the studies done by other professionals and will need to make an independent summary of the full assessment. It is important not to have this clinician finalize the full diagnostic process or the comprehensive treatment plan until all information is available.

If your son or daughter has a learning disability, he or she might become frustrated, anxious, or depressed. These secondary emotional problems can cause the behaviors of hyperactivity, distractibility, and/or impulsivity. Other problems can arise if your child or adolescent has learning disabilities and ADHD and the clinician only treats the ADHD. Because your child may now be able to sit still and attend in class, the teacher will feel that he or she should be able to learn and to keep up with the class. The learning disabilities may only now become obvious. If unrecognized, your child or adolescent could become anxious or depressed, and, despite the successful treatment of the ADHD with medication, he or she may again show behaviors of hyperactivity or distractibility in class. However, now these behaviors are due to the emotional consequences of not treating the learning disabilities and are not due to the ADHD. You and your child's clinician must constantly consider all possibilities during the treatment process.

At the risk of being accused of redundancy, may I state again that if the child or adolescent has emotional, social, or family problems, it is critical to decide whether these problems are causing the academic difficulties or are a consequence of the academic difficulties.

❖   Treatment Planning   ❖

Once the information from the family, the school, and other professionals is collected and assessed, the full clinical picture should become apparent. A multimodal treatment plan now can be developed to address each area of identified difficulty.

- If the individual has *ADHD,* the plan should include education and counseling for the individual and the family, behavioral management approaches, the use of the appropriate medication, and work with the school.

- If the individual has a *learning disability,* the plan should include special education therapy, education and counseling for the individual and the family, and work with the school.
- If the individual has *secondary* emotional, social, and/or family problems, the plan should include treatment for the primary disabilities (ADHD and possible learning disabilities), appropriate psychological interventions for the individual and the family, and work with the school.

Other interventions may be indicated, depending on the specific areas of difficulty found. Some of these interventions are done by health and/or mental health professionals; others are done by professionals who often work within the school system, such as special educators, speech and language pathologists, and occupational therapists. In each case, the clinician must collaborate with these professionals while working with the child or adolescent and with the family.

Before discussing specific approaches for helping, it would be useful to review who the various mental health professionals are. In addition, I will review the types of mental health interventions that might be considered for your son or daughter.

❖ **Mental Health Professionals** ❖

There are four basic groups of mental health professionals: psychiatrists, psychologists, social workers, and psychiatric nurses. In addition, many school systems use school or mental health counselors. Each has a core of common knowledge and skills in diagnosis and treatment as well as unique areas of expertise. Being an intelligent consumer requires that you learn all you can about the qualifications of any clinician who is going to work with your child or with your family. Don't be any less concerned about seeking the best qualified person in this field than you would be about selecting a brain surgeon.

Any of these professionals might practice one of several forms of therapy. The type of therapy offered will depend on the individual's interest and areas of training.

The *psychiatrist* is, first of all, a physician. A general psychiatrist has taken four to five years of additional specialized training after graduating from medical school. Part of this training includes experiences in psychiatric work with children and adolescents. A *child and adolescent psychiatrist* has completed the medical education and training required to become a general psychiatrist and then has taken two additional years of training in child and adolescent psychiatry. Because of her or his medical training, the general or child and adolescent psychiatrist may be best able to differentiate the biological, psychological, and social (the "biopsychosocial") aspects of a problem in the process of establishing a diagnosis. Of the mental health professionals, only psychiatrists can prescribe medication or admit patients to a hospital. All psychiatrists are trained to do individual psychotherapy; most are also trained to do group, behavioral, and family therapy. The child and adolescent psychiatrist, because of his or her additional training, may be the most qualified to do biopsychosocial diagnosis and treatment with children.

The *psychologist* may have a master's or doctorate degree. Most states require a doctorate degree for a psychologist to be licensed. The master's degree psychologist has completed a two-year graduate program beyond college. A doctorate degree is usually in clinical, counseling, school, or developmental psychology. The doctorate-level psychologist has completed at least four to six years of graduate training beyond college, including a year of special clinical training called an *internship*. Because psychologists can be trained in so many areas and because there are so many different types of internships available, any specific psychologist may have differing skills with different age groups or types of therapy. The depth and variety of training with children or adolescents also varies greatly. Psychologists have the unique training and skills to administer psychological and often educational tests. They are well trained to do evaluations and therapy. However, because the formal training and clinical experiences depend on the type of doctorate degree, type of internship, and work experience, you may want to discuss the background of your psychologist before starting an evaluation or therapy.

The *social worker* has completed college plus two years of graduate studies. After obtaining an M.S.W. degree, he or she must work under supervision for several years before being eligible to take the clinical certification examination. If this examination is passed, he or she becomes a licensed clinical social worker (L.C.S.W.). The level of diagnostic and treatment skills in working with children and adolescents depends on the social worker's additional experiences after graduation or on other postgraduate training they have sought out. The kinds of therapies offered also will be based on this required experience or other experiences. Thus being a social worker does not necessarily mean that the individual is experienced in diagnosis and treatment with children and adolescents. You need to learn what training and experiences they have had since graduation from their school of social work.

The *psychiatric nurse* may have completed a two-, three-, or four-year training program leading to a certificate as a registered nurse (R.N.) or a bachelor's degree in nursing. Some have taken a two-year master's degree program in psychiatric nursing and some have obtained the experiences by working in the field. To be certified as a clinical specialist in psychiatric nursing, he or she must have a master's or doctorate degree in psychiatric or mental health nursing or an acceptable equivalent and must pass a national examination. The psychiatric nurse with graduate school training has core knowledge and skills comparable with those of the other mental health professionals with a master's level of training. Many focus on family therapy, but many are also skilled in individual, behavioral, or group therapy. As with the social worker, you will want to know if he or she has had special training experiences with children and adolescents.

Mental health counselors form a mixed group today. Many have a master's degree and are highly qualified. Some have less training and may be less qualified. If the counselor is part of the school team, he or she can be a valuable part of the intervention program. If she or he is in private practice, ask questions about his or her qualifications and experiences.

You can see that there are several professionals within the mental health field, and within each profession practitioners have widely different levels of training and experiences. Not all are equally well trained to work with children or adolescents. I am surprised at times when I see friends search the country to find the best surgeon for a specific procedure or the best physician to treat a specific disorder, yet they take a family member to a local mental health practitioner without asking for training, qualifications, or experiences. Is the mind any less important?

It is not inappropriate to discuss a person's training, experiences, and specialty. After all, you are entrusting your child and possibly your family to him or her. It is not rude to reject a therapist and look for another if you do not feel comfortable with that person or feel that he or she does not relate well to your child or adolescent.

❖ Psychological Therapies ❖

The various behaviors of children and adolescents reflect many kinds of emotional problems. Any evaluation must look at all aspects of behavior, and, depending on the findings, specific types of therapy are recommended that best address the problems identified. Often, several problems are noted, calling for a combination of treatments. Be concerned about a mental health professional who always recommends the same form of therapy. Let me briefly review the different types of evaluations and therapy offered.

The *dynamic* or *psychoanalytic* evaluation (or "intrapsychic assessment") is done by talking with the child or adolescent. For younger children, play materials may be used as a vehicle for communicating. The evaluator looks at the interactions between internal thinking processes (basic wishes and needs, conscience, or value systems), the ability to assess the realities of the outside world, and the ability to mediate what to do. He or she explores questions related to the relative strengths of each of these processes, the coping skills available, the types of problems or conflicts the child or adolescent is struggling with, and whether all of these factors are age-appropriate or not. If conflicts are found, *individual psychoanalytically oriented psychotherapy* might be recommended.

In a *behavioral* evaluation, the clinician observes and records behaviors in an attempt to observe how the behaviors were learned and why they persist. If the behaviors are not successful or are dysfunctional, how might they be changed? What reinforces the behavior? In addition, the clinician might assess the individual's ability to handle anxiety or certain thoughts, feelings, or experiences that are causing stress and difficulty with functioning. *Behavioral therapy* might include a behavioral management program, techniques for handling anxiety better (such as *progressive relaxation therapy*), or techniques for handling feelings and thoughts better (called *cognitive-behavioral therapy*).

The *interpersonal evaluation* often involves directly observing the child or adolescent in several settings or obtaining information from people who observe him or her in these settings. How does the child interact with peers and adults? What roles does he or she play? Are there patterns of behavior that explain difficulties relating or communicating? If problems appear in these areas, *group therapy* might be recommended. If the difficulties relate to social skills, *social skill training* might be considered.

The *family* evaluation looks at family functioning. The family is seen together. What roles does the child or adolescent play? What effect does this role have on other family members? What effect do the other family members have on the child? What is the relationship between the parents, and how does this affect the family? Difficulties in these areas might lead to *family therapy* and/or to *couples therapy*.

By the time some children are evaluated, their problems have become so complex that a multiple approach is needed. The full family may be seen initially both to educate and to help parents regain control and confidence. At this time, a behavioral modification system might be introduced to assist in setting some limits on the child's or adolescent's unacceptable behaviors. Once the behavior is under control, the child or adolescent might be seen individually and the parents as a couple. The family continues to be seen together on occasion as well.

To help your child or adolescent and your family, select a competent clinician, one who is well trained, experienced, and skilled, and one you like and whom you feel you can talk to easily. Preferably, the clinician should be comfortable with more than one model of therapy and be flexible in using whichever approach is most helpful at any given time. The clinician must be knowledgeable about ADHD and the special problems of the child or adolescent with this problem and their family.

Summary

A multimodal treatment plan is necessary to treat ADHD. Your child's clinician can be the director or coordinator of this plan or can be involved in one aspect of the plan. Whatever role he or she has, it is critical that all involved with the child be aware of what the others are doing and that the efforts be coordinated. This multimodal treatment plan includes

1. Individual and family education
2. Individual, parent, and family counseling
3. Appropriate behavioral management programs
4. Appropriate use of medication

In the next few chapters, I will focus on each of these approaches.

Chapter 10

Individual and
Family Education

Many of your son's or daughter's behavioral and school problems can be confusing. These problems might reflect possible attention-deficit hyperactivity disorder (ADHD) plus the possible associated disorders. Classroom teachers might focus on the behaviors without recognizing the underlying problems; they describe only your child's inability to sit still, stay on task, or complete a task or impulsive behaviors such as interrupting or fighting. As a parent, you might repeat the concerns of the school to your clinician as well as share your personal frustrations and experiences. Often you remind the clinician that you have been talking to the teachers and to your family physician for years, only to be told that you are an "overworried parent" or that your child "will outgrow it." But, neither statement turned out to be true. The problems persisted and became worse.

Moreover, the school staff might displace their own feelings of frustration and helplessness onto you, the parent. Parents rarely, if ever, get a call from someone at the school saying, "Your child had such a great day, I would like to compliment you on being such a good parent." Instead, they receive calls telling them of their child's disruptive behaviors or of their not completing their work. The nonverbal message to the parents is "Do something about it . . . make your child behave and learn."

The children and adolescents with ADHD may also be frustrated. For them, the disabilities are not obvious. They have had only one brain throughout their life, and they do not know that it is not functioning like other people's brains. All they know is that they want to be good, they want to be successful in school, and they try as hard as the others; yet they do not succeed and they seem to get into trouble. Over time they have been accused of being bad, being lazy, not trying, or being a trouble maker. Eventually they begin to believe what they are told. They begin to feel that they are dumber than their classmates or that they are bad.

The critical first step in any multimodal approach to treatment, therefore, must be to educate the parents and then their child. This educational process may be needed for other significant individuals such as brothers and sisters, grandparents, and child care workers. Each must understand these invisible handicaps. Each must understand that, although invisible, these disabilities are just as debilitating as any other chronic handicapping condition. Each must also understand that having these problems does not mean that the child or adolescent is bad or dumb. Finally, each must understand the treatment plan.

Over the past 25 years of working with individuals with ADHD and/or learning disabilities, I have followed many of them through their childhood and adolescence, into their young-adult life. Often, I ask them to tell me which interventions were the most helpful for them and which were not. I explain that I want to learn from them so that I can better help others. The most consistent response they give me is "When you first explained who I was." Before this time, they saw themselves as dumb or bad. After this time, they began to understand their disabilities, and with this new knowledge of themselves they were able to rethink and change their self-image.

As with any chronic problem, these children and adolescents must understand their illness and how it impacts on them during each stage of life. They also must understand the models of treatment, what the treatment is suppose to accomplish, and their critical role in this treatment program. By understanding and playing an active role in what happens to them, they are more accepting of and compliant with the treatment programs.

❖ **Educational Process** ❖

The educational plan I use starts with my interpretive session with the parents. If their child has ADHD, I explain the disorder and the proposed treatment. A model for understanding ADHD is presented at the end of this chapter. If their son or daughter has a learning disability, I explain what it is, using the input→integration→memory→output model described in Chapter 4.

Before this session I review the data from the psychological and educational evaluations. If I do not understand part of the report, I call the professional who did it and ask for help. I want to be able to translate the information into a form understandable to me and to the parents. If there are emotional, social, and/or family problems, I discuss each and explain whether I see these problems as primary and a cause of the academic difficulties or as secondary and a consequence of the ADHD and/or learning disabilities. I end the session by summarizing the necessary multimodal treatment plan, who will do each part of the plan, and my specific role as part of the treatment team or as coordinator of this team.

My second session in this educational process is with the child or adolescent. I review the same materials I did with the parents. The only difference for me between meeting with a five year old, a ten year old, or a 15 year old is my style of communicating. Each must understand. I try to use material from the diagnostic sessions. For example, "You remember that you told me that when you read you often skipped words or lines. Well, that problem is because of the figure-ground difficulty we just discussed." When I describe the fidgetiness, the distractibility, or the impulsivity, they know what I am talking about.

At the end of this session I emphasize that they are not dumb or bad. I stress that we now know why they have had such difficulties in school and with life and that we can do many things to make their life better and more successful. This last statement is critical. A clinician should never tell a child or adolescent that he or she has a problem without immediately following with how the problem will be addressed and helped.

My third session is with the full family. In addition to any siblings, I encourage other significant adults to attend. If a grandparent believes that there is nothing wrong with his or her grandchild and that the problem is only that the mother is not strict enough, he or she should come. At this session, the findings and the treatment recommendations are reviewed again. This time I try to get the child or adolescent to help me: "Mary, I am not sure that I am doing a good job of explaining this problem to your brother. Can you think of an example that might help?" My goal is to educate each member of the family and to begin to change the role this child or adolescent has had in the family. He or she is not the bad one of the family or the troublemaker in school. He or she is not dumb or mentally retarded. There are reasons for the behaviors and problems and something can be done to help. It is important, also, to support the parents and siblings. The behaviors they have had to put up with should not be permitted to continue. They need to know that this child or adolescent was not just "bad" but that there were reasons for the behaviors. Once the problems are addressed, the behaviors are expected to decrease or stop. During this session, the clinician can get a better feel for the family dynamics and the types of family interventions that might be needed.

One might say that a three-session educational process is too lengthy. I find that these sessions are very valuable to the family and to me as the clincian. By the end of the last session, I have less confusion and less resistance from the parents, the siblings, and the child or adolescent with ADHD. I have built a knowledge base and a relationship that can be used throughout the treatment process. Because ADHD plus possible learning disabilities may be chronic disorders, this treatment process may go on for years, being revised for each developmental stage. In the long run, these three sessions are a most clinical and time-efficient use of effort.

❖ **Educational Process With the School** ❖

It is important that the school understand and accept the clinical findings. If the child or adolescent has ADHD, the classroom teacher will need help in working with this student. If medications are used, the teacher and others will need to know what to observe and how to relay this information to the parents and the clinician.

Some school systems in the United State used to encourage parents to see their family physician to establish the diagnosis of ADHD. Once this was done, the parents were told, "Your child has a medical disorder and, thus, we have no responsibilities." Fortunately, in September 1991, the U.S. Department of Education released a memorandum putting a stop to such actions. This document clarified the responsibility of each state and local educational agency to provide special education and related services to eligible children with ADHD.

Someone must educate you on your rights and on how to advocate for your child's needs. (Your rights are reviewed in Chapter 16.) You should also seek out one of the support organizations listed in Appendix A to help you. Your clinician might go to a meeting with you or help select someone else to go so that your needs and your child's needs are recognized and handled.

❖ Specific Education ❖
on the Use of Medication

A clinician should not use medication unless he or she believes that the child or adolescent's behaviors are due to ADHD and, thus, are neurologically based. If this is the case, the clinician must understand that ADHD is a chronic and a pervasive disorder. The clinician must believe and, therefore, educate you as parents to the following basic realities:

1. *ADHD is not just a school disability; it is a life disability.* The brain does not know the difference between 9:00 A.M. and 6:00 P.M. nor the difference between Monday and Saturday, November and August, or school days and vacations. If the clinician only treats the child's ADHD from 8:00 A.M. to 4:00 P.M. on school days, the child or adolescent may do well at school; however, he or she will continue to have difficulty within the family, doing homework, or interacting with peers. The clinician must assess the need for medication during all hours of each day and use the medication for each period of time it is needed.
2. *ADHD may persist beyond puberty, even into adulthood.* As discussed earlier, about 50% of children with ADHD will improve at

puberty; however, 50% will continue to have ADHD into adolescence. Of these adolescents, up to 70% or more may continue to have ADHD as adults. There is nothing magical about puberty. If the individual continues to have ADHD, he or she will continue to need treatment.

It is important that parents understand the concept of ADHD and the reasons for the proposed treatments. It is equally important for the child or adolescent to understand. Many parents are fearful of medication. They do not want their son or daughter to be "drugged," "sedated," or "tranquilized." It is important for you to understand that we do not use "drugs," we use "medications," and that these medications do not drug, sedate, or tranquilize your son or daughter. As you will learn in Chapter 13, these medications allow your child or adolescent to function "normally"; that is, the medication is presumed to correct a neurochemical deficit in the brain, allowing the brain to act normally. A model for understanding this concept is discussed below.

Some parents have heard partial or incorrect information, or misinformation, on some of the medications used to treat ADHD. They might have read the *Physicians' Desk Reference* (or *PDR*) and not realized that the Food and Drug Administration requires that all side effects for each medication be listed, even those that are rare. Your clinician should listen to your concerns and answer your questions. I also provide this information in Chapter 13.

Much misinformation or incorrect information was provided to parents by the mass media during the summer of 1988. During the spring of 1988, a group called the Citizens Commission on Human Rights began to attack the use of Ritalin (methylphenidate). They circulated a small booklet entitled *How Psychiatry Is Making Drug Addicts out of America's Children*. As stated in the booklet, this group was sponsored by the Church of Scientology. The Church of Scientology has had a long history of attacking the use of medications for the treatment of psychiatric disorders.

The Citizens Commission on Human Rights used a model that is not uncommon for the Church of Scientology. They announced to the media that they were filing a class-action suit against the American Psychiatric Association (representing the group of physicians most commonly prescribing Ritalin) and against CIBA-GEIGY Corporation (representing the major manufacturer of Ritalin). The media loves sensationalism. The Citizens Commission's announcement led to guest spots for their spokespersons on most of the national and local television and radio talk shows, and the print media followed up with interviews. On the talk shows, the spokespersons could and did say anything to support their views. They offered few facts and often gave incorrect data. At times they gave "information" that was partially correct or completely incorrect. Sadly, many of the viewers of these shows assumed that because the spokespersons said something on television or radio that it must be true.

The Church of Scientology had used this model in the past to gain free publicity for their views. In the fall of 1988, the Citizens Commission quietly announced to the American Psychiatric Association and to CIBA-GEIGY Coporation—but not to the media—that they would not be filing a class-action suit. The sensationalism was over. They were no longer seen on television. However, their method worked. They received a lot of free airtime and publicity. Many families heard them and became afraid of the medication or believed what they had heard.

In their booklet and in radio, television, and press interviews, the Citizens Commission on Human Rights stated that 1) Ritalin can lead to suicide, 2) Ritalin can be addictive, 3) Ritalin overdose can cause death, and 4) Ritalin is used in excess for too many children. None of these statements is correct. Each of these points is discussed in Chapter 13.

❖ Model for Understanding ❖ ADHD and the Rationale for Treatment

I would like to describe how I explain ADHD and the role of medication to parents and to their child or adolescent. The statements are based on current research. I do simplify some of the concepts to illustrate the issue, yet I believe that I am providing the best current information on ADHD and its treatment.

I need first to review what the current research strongly suggests about ADHD. All of the facts are not yet in, but the research does give us some understanding. Let me review each of the behaviors: hyperactivity, distractibility, and impulsivity. In doing this, let me do so as if you were sitting in my office and I was talking directly to you.

Hyperactivity

It is uncommon for *hyperactivity* to refer to a child or adolescent who is running around and unable to be still. The term usually refers to the individual who is fidgety. At any time the fingers are moving, the pencil is tapping, the individual is up or down out of the seat. Some part of the body seems always to be in motion.

There is an area in the brain that stimulates muscle (or motor) activity. It is in the thinking part of the brain (called the *cortex*). I call this area the "accelerator." There is another area in the lower part of the brain (called the *ascending reticular activating system*) that decides how much of these messages will get through to the muscles. I call this area the "brakes." Normally there is a balance between the accelerator and the brakes, and the brakes appear to be the controlling factor. This method of controlling muscle activity is probably for survival purposes. If you are walking down the street at night and a dog jumps out barking, you cannot say to the accelerator, "Get me out of here." You just release the brakes and take off. Later you will stop and recover by breathing hard or by your heart beating rapidly.

Using this model, it appears that children or adolescents with ADHD manifested by hyperactivity have a brake that is not working effectively. Thus the accelerator is not as controlled and the individual has an increased amount of motor activity. Current ADHD research strongly suggests that this brake does not work effectively because of a decrease in a particular neurotransmitter. The neurotransmitter that is suspected of being deficient is norepinephrine. The medications used to treat hyperactivity work by increasing the amount of norepinephrine at the nerve interface in this lower part of the brain. Once the amount of norepinephrine reaches a normal level, the brakes can work effectively, controlling the accelerator. The result is a decrease in hyperactivity. These medications, therefore, do not drug or sedate or tranquilize the individual. They make the individual "normal." These medications work much the same way insulin does for someone with diabetes. When a diabetic person is given insulin, he or she can function normally. Once the insulin is metabolized, he or she returns to being diabetic. So, too, when the proper medication is used to treat the ADHD, the individual can function normally. Once the medication is metabolized, the ADHD behaviors return.

Distractibility

First, let me review the concept of distractibility, distinguishing it from the types of internal and external distractibility described in Chapter 3. With ADHD we find a specific type of distractibility that makes it difficult for individuals to distinguish between relevant and nonrelevant stimuli in their environment. They have difficulty blocking out unimportant stimuli. Thus these nonrelevant stimuli distract them, and they have difficulty sustaining attention.

Now, let me review in a simple way the brain process for handling information when it comes into our brain through our senses. We pass this information through a "filter system." If the information is important, it is allowed to pass through to the thinking part of the brain (the cortex). If it is not important or if it can be handled at a lower level of the brain, it is monitored or processed at a lower level of the brain. In this way, the cortex is not cluttered with every stimulus that enters the brain. This filter system appears to be in the same lower area of the brain as the braking system. It is for this reason that two apparently unrelated behaviors—hyperactivity and distractibility—are often seen together.

Let me illustrate how a normal filter system works. You might be in a store and many children are yelling "Mommy" or "Daddy"; yet you only hear your child. Or if you are like me, you probably get in your car and drive home and then suddenly realize that you were daydreaming and do not know how you did not get lost or hit someone. Somehow, your brain was able to monitor important information at a lower level, freeing your cortex to think of other things.

With ADHD, the filter system (like the braking system) is not working effectively because of a decrease in the neurotransmitter norepinephrine. The medications work by increasing the amount of this neurotransmitter. Once the neurotransmitter reaches a normal level, the filter system begins to work normally. Once the filter system can work normally, these individuals can filter out unimportant stimuli. They are no longer distractible with a short attention span. They can now stay on task and block out unimportant sounds or visions in their environment.

Impulsivity

We know less about impulsivity than we do about hyperactivity or distractibility. Let me explain what we think might be the situation. When information is processed in the brain it appears to arrive at a basic "circuit board." From here it is relayed to many areas of the brain for action and then comes back to this circuit board for a reaction. In persons with impulsivity, it appears that this basic circuit board is not working effectively. There may be some "short circuits" causing the initial input to be responded to immediately. These individuals do not stop to think before they talk or act. They are impulsive.

This basic circuit board appears to be in the same lower part of the brain as the brakes or the filter system, and it is believed to not be working effectively because of a decrease in the amount of the neurotransmitter norepinephrine. The medications increase the production of this neurotransmitter in this area of the brain, allowing the circuit board to work normally. Thus the individual is less impulsive and better able to reflect before talking or acting.

This concept of a braking system, a filter system, and a circuit board is simplistic. It uses poetic license with neurophysiology by simplifying it. However, it is not an incorrect description. It is symbolic enough and close enough to what the current research suggests about ADHD that parents and their children can understand the problem and the rationale for treatment. I find that after explaining the model, I can work on the treatment plans by using these words to shortcut lengthy conversations: "The filter system is working better but not fully. He is still somewhat distractible. We should increase the amount of the medication."

This model also stresses the neurological basis for ADHD. It clarifies that the medication is specific and explains the reasons for using it. This model decreases the concerns parents have that they are drugging their child to make the teacher happy or to make it easier for him or her to live in the family. The concept of making the child or adolescent "normal" and the analogy to diabetes is an important one for parents and for the child or adolescent to understand.

 # Summary

A critical part of any multimodal treatment plan for individuals with ADHD is education. This educational process must include the individual with ADHD, parents, and family. Often, this educational process is all that is needed to help the individual and the family move ahead with the other parts of the treatment plan for ADHD and any associated disorders. If more education is needed, individual, parent, and/or family counseling may be indicated. I will discuss these approaches in the following chapters.

Chapter 11

Individual, Parent, and Family Counseling

The individual and family educational processes described in the previous chapter often result in emotional and behavioral changes with everyone and an improvement in the behavior of the child or adolescent with attention-deficit hyperactivity disorder (ADHD). Parents begin to be assertive advocates for their son or daughter, resulting in more appropriate programs within the school system. They begin to understand their child or adolescent and begin to change their parenting behaviors.

If, after these efforts, you and your clinician decide that you, your child, or your whole family needs further help, specific therapy may be necessary. Behavioral management techniques might be needed. One parent or both parents might need help with their emotional difficulties or in working through their resistance or struggles with the problems. The child or adolescent might need help with his or her emotional or behavioral difficulties or with denial or noncompliance.

It might be necessary for parents to enter couples therapy, for the child or adolescent to enter individual dynamic or behavioral therapy, or for the family to start in family therapy. It is important to delay such decisions until this point in the process so that you and your clinician can assess if the problems have been improved or resolved through the educational process or the initial counseling efforts along with the use of appropriate medications.

Whichever form of clinical intervention is started, it is critical that your clinician consistently keep in mind the impact the ADHD and possible associated disorders can have on both your child or adolescent and your family. It is equally important to understand how these disorders can impact on the treatment process.

❖   **Clinical Work With the Child**   ❖
or Adolescent

If, after the educational process, better school accommodations, and the use of appropriate medications, your child or adolescent continues to have emotional or behavioral difficulties, individual therapy might be indicated. Dynamic psychotherapy or cognitive-behavioral therapy might be considered. The techniques are the same as those used for other emotional or behavioral disorders.

The first phase of therapy continues to focus on education. The child or adolescent needs to understand his or her disabilities and the impact they have on every aspect of life. With this new knowledge, the individual might try to understand the past and the difficulties experienced. By doing this, his or her self-image and self-esteem can improve.

Often children and adolescents do not see their role in school, peer, and family problems. The therapist might try to review recent events in an effort to help them learn about their behaviors and how they impact on others. Once they accept their role in what happens to them, they need to explore and to learn alternative models of behavior, as well as alternative coping strategies.

For children and adolescents with emotional problems manifested by a poor self-image, anxiety, and/or depression, the above approaches are helpful. For those with disruptive or antisocial behavioral problems, group or family therapy along with a behavioral management system might be considered.

At every stage of therapy in any setting, it is important for the clinician to be aware of the impact the ADHD and any associated disorders can have on understanding, performance, or interactions. It is equally important that the clinician understand how the ADHD and any associated disorders can impact on the therapeutic setting and process.

❖   **Social Skill Training**   ❖

Social skills needed for social competence include physical factors (such as eye contact and posture), social responsivity (such as sharing), and interactional skills (such as initiating and maintaining conversation). Before a child or adolescent starts in a social skill training program, it is important for the clinician to identify the individual's areas of social incompetence and the specific skills that appear to be missing.

There are many programs described in the literature for doing social skill training. In general, they focus on a series of steps. The first step involves helping the child or adolescent to develop a sensitivity for his or her social problems. This step is critical. Because of their impulsivity and inattention, some children with ADHD have only limited awareness of their socialization difficulties and may deny or project the source of their problems onto others. The second step involves having the child or adolescent generate alternative solutions for the identified problems. Here, the clinician and other group members can be of help. The third step involves helping the child or adolescent step-by-step through the process of learning the newly identified solution to the problem. Role playing and practice are important ways of learning these new solutions. The final step is to help the child or adolescent link the new knowledge to past events and difficulties as well as to future events. The child or adolescent is then encouraged to try out the new social skills in new settings and to report back on successes and failures.

❖   **Clinical Work With the Parent**   ❖

The problems of children and adolescents with ADHD are not limited to the behaviors of hyperactivity, distractibility, and/or impulsivity. Thus even if medication controls these behaviors, other behaviors may need to be addressed. There may be other difficulties such as aggression, oppositional defiant behavior, conduct disturbances, academic difficulties, low self-esteem, depression, and poor peer relationships.

Therapeutic work with parents might focus on those perceptions of their child or adolescent that have not shifted with the educational process or on parents' perceptions of themselves that are based on past experiences with their son or daughter with ADHD. A cognitive therapy approach might help with these difficulties.

Parents might have emotional or behavioral problems of their own or secondary to the stresses of raising a child or adolescent with ADHD. Specific individual psychotherapy or the use of specific medications might be useful.

If there is marital stress, couples therapy might be indicated. This work might include forming a shared understanding of the child or adolescent with ADHD and his or her needs and understanding how the previous lack of such knowledge or understanding created stress between the parenting couple. The couple needs to work together to develop family strategies to handle the disruptive behaviors of the son or daughter with ADHD and to find positive ways to help this son or daughter, as well as any other children.

Some parents need help being their son's or daughter's advocate with the school system and with other activities. They need help in finding the necessary information and parent support groups. Furthermore, they may need an advocate to work with them who knows the system and knows how to help parents negotiate their way through the school system.

❖ Clinical Work With the Family ❖

Sometimes the family is under so much stress and is so dysfunctional that family therapy is needed before any educational or other therapeutic process can be considered. The early phases of this therapy might focus on giving the parents back the controls and on helping the child or adolescent with ADHD feel safe not being in control. Specific behavioral management approaches must be started. Later, when the family is functioning better, other clinical interventions can be considered as the needs are clarified.

Family therapy can be helpful in changing the family members' perceptions and expectations of the child or adolescent with ADHD. Sibling conflicts can be addressed. The focus is often on changing unacceptable behaviors and on strengthening the positive relationships between family members. As siblings learn to understand and as they see positive changes within the family, they can become advocates for their brother or sister with ADHD at school, in the neighborhood, and in community activities. They can help with problems of peer behavior and peer rejection. A specific model for changing unacceptable behaviors in the family is addressed in Chapter 12.

❖   **Working With the School**   ❖

It is hoped that the use of appropriate medication will lessen or stop the hyperactivity, distractibility, and/or impulsivity. If so, the classroom teacher needs to understand the medications, how they work, what side effects might occur, how to observe behaviors, and how to communicate with the clinician managing the medication. If the use of medication is less than successful, the classroom teacher will need to provide special efforts to help the student in school.

If the child or adolescent with ADHD also has an associated learning disability, it is hoped that the school will have identified this disability and that the appropriate special educational interventions and classroom accommodations are in place. If the school has not identified the learning disability or started the necessary programs for your child, you may need help in getting the school to do so.

There is much new literature on the roles of the classroom teacher in working with a student who has ADHD. If the student also has learning disabilities, additional interventions will be necessary. Such efforts focus on four areas: 1) establishing the best learning environment, 2) giving instructions and assignments, 3) modifying unacceptable behaviors, and 4) enhancing self-esteem.

The classroom environment should be modified to address the hyperactivity and/or distractibility. The student should sit near the teacher's desk to increase the teacher's awareness and control. The student should be seated in the front of the class with his or her back to the rest of the class, thus minimizing the amount of visual stimulation. The student should be surrounded with good role models, preferably students who will not get pulled into inappropriate behavior. Distracting stimuli, such as air conditioners, open windows or doors, and high-traffic areas, should be minimized. Transitions and changes should be handled with awareness that these activities might be difficult. The student with ADHD might need more structure and supervision in the hall, at lockers, at lunch, or on field trips.

When giving instructions or assignments, the teacher should maintain eye contact with the student and make the information clear and concise. There should be consistency with daily instructions and expectations. The teacher should be sure that the student understands the directions before beginning the task. If necessary, he or she should repeat the instructions. The student should be made to feel comfortable when seeking help. It is helpful to require a daily assignment notebook in which the student writes down all assignments each day. The teacher signs the notebook to confirm that the assignments are correct, and the parents sign to show that the work was done.

To modify behavior, the rules of the classroom should be clear and known. If the student breaks one of the rules, the teacher should remain calm, state the infraction of the rule, and avoid debating or arguing with the student. It is helpful to have preestablished responses or consequences for inappropriate behaviors. The consequences should be presented quickly and consistently. It is important that the teacher avoid ridicule and criticism.

Building or rebuilding self-esteem is important. The teacher should reward more than punish. Any and all good behavior and performances should be praised immediately. Ways should be found to encourage the child. If the child or adolescent has difficulty, it is important that the teacher find a way of reestablishing contact and trust so that new solutions can be found and tried.

❖   **Summary**   ❖

After the impact of individual and parent education and the use of appropriate medications are assessed, individual, parent, or family counseling may be necessary. It is essential to work closely with the school at each step of the interventions.

The specific approach will depend on the assessed need. It is important that one clinician coordinate all efforts to be sure that each identified problem is addressed. Whatever form of individual, couples, family, or other therapy is used, it is important that your clinician understand the impact of the ADHD and any associated disorders on the problems being addressed.

Chapter 12

Behavioral Approaches to Treatment

I would like to teach you a model for assessing behaviors within your family and for setting up your own behavioral program to change unacceptable behaviors. It should work. If it does not, you may need to seek help from a professional. Let me describe the types of problems, the models for clarifying what needs to be changed, the basic model for demanding change, and additional models that might be used along with the basic model.

In an initial evaluation session with parents, a clinician might hear them describe their son as a tyrant who must have his way or all hell breaks loose with screaming, throwing things, hitting his brother or sister, messing up his room, or "something." Later, the clinician meets this "tyrant"—a four-foot, 70-pound little boy who could be picked up and carried under one arm. Where is the monster?

Then the clinician begins to work with the family and soon finds out. This child's behavior does dominate the family. The parents avoid too many confrontations because they do not want to face the consequences. They "look the other way" until pushed so far that they have to react. By that time, feeling helpless, the parents' only possible reaction often is anger. They yell, hit the child, or give out a punishment like "no television for one week," but then have to back down because they have no way to enforce it or because enforcing it leads to more confrontations and fights.

As the evaluation progresses, the clinician may gain clues or clarify the dynamics within the child or within the family that explain the behaviors. What is more likely to occur is that the clinician cannot clarify the underlying issues but can see that something has to be done and quickly. One has to "put out the fire" before an in-depth assessment can be considered. What is clear is that the child is in control and the parents are not in control or are out of control. What may also be clear is that the parents disagree, and, rather than supporting each other, they are split and fighting with each other. This situation in the family produces anxiety for the child and is not compatible with healthy psychosocial development. This situation is also dysfunctional for the parents and other members of the family.

Perhaps the clinician can see patterns. Without meaning to do so, the parents are reinforcing the very behaviors they do not want. The child acts badly and gets a lot of attention, negative attention. The parents get upset and this proves to the child that she or he can control one part of the world, the family. This, along with getting what the child wants, is the reward for bad behavior. The other children see the parents forced to give in. They become angry. Soon, they may learn that the only way to get attention or to get what one wants is to be bad.

Whatever the dynamics or initial cause, the family dysfunction must be corrected. The parents must regain control. Children with attention-deficit hyperactivity disorder (ADHD) must feel that they can be controlled. These changes are essential for the whole family. Negative control of parents is unhealthy and unproductive. These children must learn more acceptable behavioral patterns before they start using these negative behaviors at school, with peers, or in the community.

Once the behaviors are in control, children and adolescents with ADHD can begin to learn new and better techniques to function within the family and to cope with stress. Parents and children can rework styles of interacting and roles within the family. First comes the behavioral changes and then comes such awareness and insight.

It is not uncommon to find that the same child or adolescent who is out of control at home is functioning very well in school, at friends' houses, or when playing with friends away from home. Sunday School teachers, activity leaders, and sports coaches might think this child is well behaved, a perfect lady or gentleman. Hence, one might assume that the behavioral difficulties are not neurologically driven; otherwise they would occur in every setting. If the behaviors are only expressed at home, it is possible that they reflect family dynamics or conflict. It is also possible that the child or adolescent holds in his or her frustration and anger all day so as not to get into trouble and then lets it all out at home where it is safe to do so. Another possibility is that the child has ADHD and is on the appropriate medication and doing well during the hours the medication is working; however, he or she is not taking the medication during times other than school hours. The addition of the medication for evenings and weekends might lead to a significant improvement in home behaviors. If the behaviors are only seen while the child is at home, a behavioral management program might be needed just for the family.

On the other hand, the clinician might observe that the negative or aggressive behaviors are seen in school, with peers, during activities, and at home. Often this picture is associated with ADHD. In this situation, the clinician should consider the possibility that the neurologically driven behaviors of hyperactivity, distractibility, and/or impulsivity are causing or contributing to the difficulties. Once medication is started, the behaviors might decrease or stop. If not, the behavioral management program will have to include school and activities outside the home as well.

❖ Behavioral Management Concepts ❖

Any behavioral plan must be based on two important concepts of learning theory. First, you are more likely to succeed in changing behavior by rewarding what is desired than by punishing what is undesired. Second, for a plan to work, your responses to acceptable and to unacceptable behaviors must be consistent and must occur each time. Inconsistent responses or inconsistent response patterns may reinforce the negative behavior.

As parents you must learn that there is no right or wrong way to raise children. You must collaborate in developing a plan that you are comfortable with and agree on. Once decided on, the plan must be practiced in a consistent and persistent way.

Initially, you must be omnipotent. No more reasoning, bargaining, bribing, threatening, or trying to provoke guilt. Parents make the rules. Parents enforce the rules. Parents' decisions are final. You must learn that if you "step into the arena" and agree to debate or argue with your child, you will lose. If a parent says it is time to go to sleep and a child says, "But can I stay up 15 minutes more," the answer must be, "I did not ask you what time you wanted to go to sleep. I said it is bedtime." Argue about the 15 minutes and it becomes 20 minutes, and then 30 minutes. Soon, the parents' frustration and anger will result in fighting. Later in the plan there can be flexibility, but not initially.

Developing the Initial Intervention Strategy

Initially, parents are usually overwhelmed. They have exhausted their choices of actions. They may feel helpless and like failures as parents. If there are two parents, there may be stress between them caused by disagreement on how to handle the behaviors or by blaming the other for the problems. Try to follow this plan. If you are too worn out or overwhelmed, seek professional help.

The first step is to collect data on your observations of the behaviors. Each parent should collect data separately. The differences between the two will be very useful. Don't be embarrassed by what you do. Record what really happens without worrying what someone will think. We already know that things are not working well. Just record your experiences so you can begin to change things.

You will need a structure to collect these data. The easiest model to use is an "ABC" chart. You record three things: the behavior (B), the antecedent to the behavior (A), and the consequences of the behavior (C). The chart will look something like

Date/Time	Antecedent	Behavior	Consequence

A typical entry might read like

Date/Time	Antecedent	Behavior	Consequence
Monday 4:30 P.M.	Don't know; not there	John hit sister; she hit him back	Told both to go to room
6:00 P.M.	Talking to Mary	John teased her; she cried	Yelled at John
9:00 P.M.	Told John to get ready for bed	Refused to take bath, get in PJs; yelled at me when told	Took 30 minutes of reminding; finally hit him and he went to take bath

Each parent may have different lists. In part, this reflects when each is home and with the child or adolescent. One may be the firm disciplinarian and the other the easygoing, "give them another chance" type. Each parent will see and list different things. Each has different experiences and expectations. Father may come home at 6:00 or 6:30 P.M. looking forward to being with the children and playing with them. Mother may be frustrated and short of temper, having had it by then, and wanting the kids to be quiet and to get their homework and other chores done so that they can go to bed.

Neither parent is right or wrong. The important goal is that both parents agree on their expectations and be consistent in asking that they be met. Consistency is the key. Inconsistency reinforces the behavior; consistency stops the behavior.

Certain patterns should become clear for each column and for overall behaviors. Certain antecedents lead to certain behaviors. The consequences that follow the same behaviors are inconsistent: one parent gets mad and yells at everything, or other family members seem to get punished as much as the child who caused the problems. A common theme is that when children do not get what they want or are asked to do something they do not want to do, they misbehave.

Once the data are collected, they are analyzed and patterns are looked for. The first task is to define clearly the unacceptable behaviors that need to be changed. Often parents start with a long list of behaviors. Once the data are studied, the behaviors can be clustered into two or three major areas. By doing this, you will not be as overwhelmed. You are not dealing with an impossible list of problems, but can focus on a few major areas.

Frequently, the unacceptable behaviors fall into three basic groups:

- Physical abuse (hitting sibling, hitting parent, hurting a pet, damaging property, etc.)
- Verbal abuse (yelling at sibling, yelling at parent, teasing, cursing or other unacceptable words, threatening someone, etc.)
- Noncompliance (not listening to what is said, not doing a requested chore, defying a parent's request, etc.)

Once the behaviors are identified, it is useful to study the relationship between the antecedents and the behaviors. Look for themes: the behaviors are more likely to occur if the child is tired, hungry, or about to be sick; the behaviors are more likely to occur during the first hour after coming home from school; the behaviors are more likely to occur when he or she is off of medication; or the behaviors appear to relate to the child's learning disabilities or sensory integrative disorder. These themes will be useful in helping the child or adolescent understand why he or she has difficulty and in helping you know when to be most alert to the possibility of problems.

Setting up the Initial Program

Once you have a clearer idea of the behaviors that need to be changed, a plan can be developed. Define the behaviors as clearly as possible and work out a consequence that can be imposed consistently. Work out the plan in great detail, then introduce it to the family. The plan should be for all siblings. Even if the other children or adolescents do not cause problems, it will not affect them negatively to be part of the program. It might benefit them by rewarding them for their good behavior. It might have been that the "bad" child took so much attention that the "good" child was ignored or not thanked for being good. This plan will help you remember to reward good behaviors. If a sibling is provoking or encouraging the negative behavior, it will become clear if he or she also is on the plan.

As parents, you need to understand that there are several basic principles to reversing the pattern of punishing bad behavior and usually ignoring or only occasionally rewarding good or positive behavior. This plan will reward positive behaviors and withhold rewards for negative behaviors. Further, you will have preplanned responses that can be used every time. Your child or adolescent cannot catch you off guard, making you feel helpless and therefore angry. Each time a behavior occurs there will be the same response from either parent.

Let me illustrate this point about consistency. Suppose a boy hits his sister five times in a week. On one occasion his mother was in such a rush that she yelled at him but did nothing else about it. On another occasion, she was tired and did not want to deal with him so she pretended not to see what happened. The other three times she did punish him. Now, if this child gives up hitting his sister because mother tells him to, he has to give up hitting her 100% of the time. If he continues to hit her, he has a 40% chance of getting away with it. He would be a fool to give up the behavior. If a parent is consistent, the behavior will stop. If the parent is anything less than consistent, the behavior might persist or get worse.

The basic plan can be divided into 3 steps:

Step 1.   Divide the day into parts. For example, on a typical school day there will be three parts: 1) from the time the child or adolescent gets up until he or she leaves for school, 2) from the time he or she returns from school until the end of the evening meal, and 3) from the end of this meal until bedtime. Weekend or summer days can be divided into four parts by using meals as the dividers: 1) from the time the child or adolescent wakes up until the end of breakfast, 2) from the end of breakfast to the end of lunch, 3) from the end of lunch to the end of dinner, and 4) from the end of dinner until bedtime.

Step 2.   Make a list of the child's or adolescent's unacceptable behaviors. This list should be brief and limited to the major problems. If the basic three noted earlier are used, a list might read:

1. No physical abuse (define in detail: no hitting sister, pulling cat's tail, kicking mother, breaking toys, etc.).
2. No verbal abuse (define in detail: no cursing, calling someone "stupid," teasing, etc.).
3. No noncompliance (define in detail: no refusing to do what you are told to do). For younger children, the term *not listening* might be used. Make it clear that you will request they stop the behavior several times. Then you will say, "If I have to ask you again, I will call it *noncompliance*." Any behavior continuing after this warning is called *noncompliance*. In this way the child or adolescent can never say, "But, you never told me I had to do this."

Step 3. The purpose of the plan is to reward positive behaviors. Negative behaviors are not mentioned as such. The child or adolescent can earn one point for each behavior he or she does not do during a unit of time. Later we will talk about "time out." With time out, too, the focus is on the positive and not the negative; thus the wording is important. The parent says, "What you did is so unacceptable in this family that you must go to your room and think about the need to change what you do." The parent does not say, "Go to you room," with the connotation that doing so is punishment.

The child can earn points by not doing the unacceptable behaviors. He or she can earn one point for each negative behavior not done. For example, suppose a boy gets up in the morning, does all of his chores, and gets to breakfast on time. He does not hit anyone, but he does call his sister "stupid." As he leaves for school his parent would say, "I am pleased that you earned two points this morning. You followed all rules and you did not hit anyone. I wish I could have given you the third point but you did call your sister a name and that is *verbal abuse*." This parent might then say to the sister, "I am happy that you earned all three of your points. Thank you for not calling your brother a name when he called you one." Remember, behavior is changed by rewarding what you want, not by punishing what you do not want.

A book or chart should be available and the points recorded. If the child is too young to understand points, a calendar or chart can be used and stars pasted on, or a jar can be filled with marbles to represent each point earned.

Each part of the day is handled in the same way. In the model with three units of time during school days and four units of time on the weekend, the maximum number of points that can be earned on a school day is nine and the maximum each weekend day is 12. The total for a week will be 69. These points can be used in three ways: a daily reward, a weekly reward, and a special reward. The points are counted daily, then continue to be counted weekly or accumulatively. The child or adolescent should participate in developing the rewards. Parents make the final decisions but keep in mind the request. If the child or adolescent says, "This is stupid. I won't do it," the parent replies, "The plan starts tomorrow. Either you suggest what you might like to work toward or I will make the decisions for you."

Each reward must be individualized for each member of the family, and each must be compatible with the family's style and philosophy. Rewards that involve interpersonal experiences are preferred to material rewards. The daily reward could be an additional half hour of TV watched with a parent, being able to stay up 30 minutes later, reading a book or playing a game with a parent, or 30 minutes of special time with one parent.

The weekly reward might be going to a movie, going out to eat with the family, or having a friend sleep over. Points are counted from Saturday morning to Friday night; thus you know if the child or adolescent has enough points before the weekend starts. In this way, a babysitter can be lined up before any family activity. In the past, your son or daughter might have been impossible all week, but he or she would still go out with the family on the weekend. Now, this child stays home and your other children go out.

A special reward might be something important that must be worked toward. A new toy or a special trip might be selected. It should take a month or more to accumulate enough points for this reward.

For the daily and weekly rewards, set an initial goal of 80% of the maximum number of points that can be earned. After a month of success (which might take several months to reach), the goal can be raised to 90%. It is best not to set the goal at 100%. No one can be perfect all of the time. Any negative behavior early in the day or week could destroy all hope of a reward and the child or adolescent might give up.

For the plan described above, the child or adolescent would need seven points each weekday evening to get the daily reward (80% of nine points). He or she would need 55 points by Friday night for the weekend reward (80% of 69 points).

Time out. Before starting the plan, define which behaviors will be considered so unacceptable to the family that they will result in the child not earning a point plus being removed from the family for a limited time so that he or she can think about the need to change this behavior. I always use this consequence for physical abuse. Other behaviors might be included. For the young child, 15 minutes is appropriate; for the older child or adolescent, 30 minutes is best.

This time is to be spent quietly thinking about what happened and why he or she needs to change. The child's or adolescent's room can be used if it is not filled with TV, stereo, games, and other pleasurable distractions. If his or her room cannot be used, a guest room or laundry room might be best. The door is to be closed and the child is to be quiet. Each time he or she opens the door or yells or throws something, the timer is reset to zero and the 15 or 30 minutes starts again. The child or adolescent soon learns that unless he or she is quiet and cooperative, a 15-minute time out can last for hours.

Time out can be used away from home as well. If you are at a restaurant and it is safe to do so, take the child or adolescent to the car. If concerned, a parent might want to stand near the car and watch. If in a shopping center, try to find a safe place for the child to sit. Tell him or her that you will return in 15 (or 30 minutes). If concerned, the parent can stand away from the child or adolescent and watch during the time.

For the plan to work, it must be exact as to expectations, behaviors that are rewarded, and consequences. Once initiated, the child or adolescent will find loopholes. The parents must be smarter than their son or daughter and close each loophole quickly. A common example is time out. A boy might be home with his mother. He is told to go to his room and refuses. He might defy his mother, run around the room, and dare her to chase him or run out of the house. If this happens, it is not good for his mother to chase him or drag him to his room.

The plan must be developed and explained in advance. The child or adolescent knows that this plan will be implemented the minute he or she refuses to go to the assigned room for time out. This plan can have two parts:

1. The parent will announce a time that the child is expected to be in the room (such as three minutes from the time that the parent informs the child to go to the room). After that time, he or she will need to spend two additional minutes in the room for every minute it takes to get to the room. This means that if the child or adolescent does not go to the room until father comes home two hours later, he or she will need to spend four additional hours in the room. This time cannot be counted after bedtime; thus it is spent in the room the next day, perhaps after school. Sometimes, the child or adolescent spends all of a weekend day making up the time needed because he or she tested the parent earlier. Soon, he or she learns to listen.

2. The second part of the plan is for the child or adolescent to know that during the time he or she refuses to go to the assigned room a second thing will happen. The parent will say, "I will always love you dearly. However, when you abuse me as a parent, I do not choose to parent you." This means that the parent will not talk to the child or adolescent or interact in any way. When mealtime comes, a place is set for everyone in the family but this person. If the child wants to eat, he or she must make his or her own meal and sit somewhere else. If the parent was to carpool to a meeting or sports practice or game, it will not be done. The child will have to face the consequences of not attending. If the behavior persists until bedtime, the parent will not respond to the child or adolescent nor put him or her to bed. Once the son or daughter goes to the room to spend the quiet time, parenting starts again.

Some parents find that the, "I love you but if you abuse me as a parent I chose not to parent you" approach too painful to consider. I remind these parents that allowing the unacceptable behaviors is more painful and potentially harmful to the child than the model suggested.

There are other loopholes children will find. For physical abuse, the child or adolescent does not earn a point and goes to a quiet room to think; thus the events are stopped. What about verbal abuse? For the first event, he or she will not earn a point. What does the parent do for the remainder of the time in this time period if this child or adolescent is verbally abusive again. I suggest that for the second occurrence, he or she must go to the quiet room for 15 to 30 minutes to think about the fact that such behavior is not acceptable in the family and he or she must change. What to do for noncompliance once the child does not earn a point is harder to handle. What do parents do when the toys still need to be put away or a bath is still needed? Later in this chapter, several alternative plans are described.

This reward-point system plus time out system will work. The key is to be consistent. You must be encouraged to develop the plan and to implement it. Your child will test the system, but, if you stick to it, the behaviors will improve. To some parents' surprise, once the external controls work and the child or adolescent functions better, he or she is happier, not more frustrated. However, once the behaviors improve, the plan must be continued. If stopped too soon, the behaviors will return.

Setting up the Second Phase of the Plan

The goal of this second phase of intervention is to help the child or adolescent internalize the controls. The first phase provided external controls. Now, the effort shifts to helping the child or adolescent build these controls into his or her behavioral patterns. The first phase continues; however, now a more interactive rather than omnipotent approach is used by parents.

Once the unacceptable behaviors are under better control, *reflective talking* can be introduced. Initially, these discussions are held after the fact. The best time might be at night while sitting on the child's bed, talking with him or her. For example, perhaps a boy has been in a fight or a yelling match. He has spent time in the quiet room. Later in the day one of his parents sits with him in private and discusses what happened: "Fred, I am sorry you had so much trouble this afternoon. I love you and I do not like being angry *with your behavior* or having to ask you to remove yourself from the family. What do you think we can do to stop such things from happening?"

Let him talk. At first he may only make angry accusations of unfairness or of others causing the trouble. The parent might respond, "I don't know if your brother was teasing you before you hit him or not. I wasn't there. But, let's suppose that he did. What else could you have done? By hitting him you got into trouble and he did not. There must be a better way. Maybe you could have told me what you thought he was doing." Such conversations may have to occur many times before the child or adolescent begins to think about his or her behavior and to consider alternative solutions to problems. It is important that the parents not only point out the behavior but offer alternative solutions.

Gradually, you will be able to point out themes: "You know, Mary, I notice that you're most likely to get into trouble right after you come home from school. Do you suppose that you hold in all of your problems all day so that you won't get in trouble and then let them out the first time you are upset at home? If so, maybe we can do something to help. Maybe, as soon as you come home you and I can sit in the kitchen, have a snack, and talk. Maybe if you tell me about your day and the problems you'll feel better and won't have to let out your feelings in a way that gets you in trouble."

Soon you will be able to do the reflective thinking before the fact: "John, you and I both have learned that if you keep playing with your brother once the teasing starts, there will be a fight. Do you remember what we talked about? What else could you do?" or "Alice, you are forcing me to be a policeperson and to yell at you or punish you. I don't like doing that. I'd rather enjoy being with you than yelling at you or punishing you. Why do you think you force me to be a policeperson? Remember what we talked about the other night? Do you want to try some of the ideas we talked about?" Gradually, the child or adolescent will begin to try the new behaviors.

Your child can learn from hearing you openly discuss feelings and thoughts. Let the child understand how you feel—angry, sad, afraid, worried. You can role model how to handle these feelings. "I am so angry with what you did that I cannot talk to you. I am going into the other room to calm down. Later, we can talk." Not only will you feel more in control, but you will have demonstrated a way to handle angry feelings.

It is important for parents to begin to explain or role model acceptable ways for their son or daughter to handle feelings. Many families are quick to tell their children how they may not show anger or sadness or disappointment, but they do not teach them acceptable ways of showing these feelings. Anger is a normal feeling and children and adolescents must learn how to handle these feeling in an acceptable way in the family. Can they yell as long as they do not curse? Can they stamp their feet or slam the door as long as they do not break anything? Watch out for confusing messages. One parent in the family yells or throws things when angry. The other parent pouts or goes to a room alone when angry. But, when the child gets angry and starts to yell, he or she is told, "You may not do that." If he or she walks off pouting, the parent says, "You come back here. I am talking to you." It is acceptable for families to have different rules for the adults and the children. However, parents must then teach their children or adolescents what are acceptable ways for them to express feelings in the family.

❖   **Additional Models**   ❖

In addition to the basic plan, other concepts can be added to address specific problems. These plans may work best with issues of noncompliance. What do you do after the child or adolescent has not earned a point, yet the requested behavior is still required? The basic concepts are the same: the parents are in control, and the rules and consequences are consistent and persistent.

Handling Chores

To avoid any confusion about chores or other duties expected by the family, you must make a detailed list of expectations. Individual chores might include putting dirty clothes in the hamper, making one's bed, and picking things up off of the floor. Family chores might include setting the table, loading or emptying the dishwasher, and vacuuming. Place the list in an obvious place. Clarify if these chores are to be rewarded by money or if they are expected as part of family responsibility. If the family chores are to be shared on different days, make a clear list of what each child is to do each day, "Alice clears the table on even number days, and Charlie clears the table on odd number days."

If the chores are expected and are not done, what will be the consistent consequence? What can you do if the child "forgets" or does not do an expected chore? Should you continue to nag and then shout? Several models are suggested below. Each gives the parents the controls. If a task is not done, there is a clear consequence. The choice is for the child or adolescent. If he or she does the chore there is the expected reward. If he or she does not do the chore there is the expected consequence.

The "maid service." Tell your child that all "parent services" are not supplied free of charge. If chores are not done by a set time, you will do them, but not for free. Make a list of the chores. Set a reasonable fee for each chore. Be realistic for the age and financial resources of the child or adolescent. For example, 25 cents for making the bed, 50 cents for picking up things from the bedroom floor, and 50 cents for putting the bike in the garage. Then, stop arguing, reminding, or nagging the child. If the chore is done by the preset time, fine. If it is not done, do the chore without comment. At the end of each day or week, submit a bill for the service. If the child gets an allowance, you might present a bill at the end of the week; for example:

Allowance	$5.00
Maid service	3.75
Balance due	1.25

Your child might get upset and ask how lunch drinks or snacks are to be bought. You reply, "Think about that next week when you decide not to do a chore." If your child does not get an allowance, use birthday or savings money. If there is no such money or if your child owes you more than the allowance, give him or her specific work details to earn the money owed: "I will pay you $2.00 per hour to clean the garage. You owe me $3.00, so I expect you to work one-and-a-half hours this weekend."

No more getting angry. No more reminding. No more fights. The child has only two options now—do the chores and get the rewards or not do the chores and pay someone else to do them.

The "Sunday box."   Set up a "box" in a secure place. A closet or room that can be locked or the trunk of a car will do. Make it clear that, after a predetermined time each day, any items left where they should not be (such as toys, bike, books, coat, shoes, etc.) will be placed in the box and that the box will not be emptied until Sunday morning. This means that if a favorite game or bike or piece of sports equipment is left out or not put away, it is lost until Sunday. If the objects are clothes or shoes and cannot be done without, the child or adolescent must pay a fee to retrieve them early.

The Sunday box worked so well in one family that a wife placed her husband on the plan. His clothes, work papers, or other things that had been left lying around disappeared into the Sunday box.

Handling Property Damage

The initial response to property damage by a child will be based on the plan in place. If this behavior is called *physical abuse,* he or she will not earn a point and must spend time in a quiet room thinking. If a larger consequence is needed, make the child pay to repair or to replace the item. The money could come out of his or her allowance; if the amount is large, the money might come out in installments until the debt is paid off, or the money could come from the child's savings account, if one exists. If this model for payment is not possible because your child does not have a savings account, give him or her a way to earn the money. Assign tasks that are not regular chores (such as cutting the grass, washing clothes, washing the kitchen floor, and cleaning the garage) and pay by the hour. The first time a child gets angry and kicks over and breaks a $50.00 lamp and then learns that he or she must work for 25 hours at $2.00 an hour to pay for the damage may be the first time that he or she starts to think before acting. And, this is the goal, getting the child or adolescent to stop before acting and to think about the consequences of the behavior.

Handling Dawdling

Many parents reinforce dawdling by reminding, nagging, yelling, screaming, and then, in anger, doing the task with or for their child. All this does is teach the child that he or she can get away with dawdling, can force the parents to help, or can make the parents upset. Instead, you must define the limits for a behavior and establish clear consequences for overstepping those limits.

For example, a girl may not get dressed on time. She is not openly oppositional, but she is so busy playing or looking out the window that tasks just never get done. As the time for the school bus gets closer she has not yet dressed or eaten because she is dawdling and playing. As a parent, you probably go into the bedroom, yell at her, and quickly dress her so she'll have time to eat and catch the bus. She has succeeded in getting you upset and angry and in getting you to help her. It is important in this situation to consider whether the difficulty in getting dressed is related to a learning disability (such as a sequence, organization, or motor disability), a sensory integrative disorder, or ADHD behaviors present because the child is not on medication during these hours.

For this type of behavior, you might first establish the rules. If, for example, your child is expected to be ready to leave for the bus by 7:40, tell him or her that "the kitchen is open until 7:30. You must be dressed to enter. If you come in before 7:15, I will make you a hot breakfast. If you come in after 7:15, you may have cold cereal. After 7:30, no food will be served; you will have to go to school hungry."

But what do you do if it is 7:40 and your child is still not dressed? For older children and adolescents, you can tell them that if they miss the bus or car pool, you will not take them to school. Thus, unless they can walk or take public transportation, they will not be able to go to school. Perhaps they will take a taxi, but they will have to pay for it. Further, tell them that you will not write a note if they are late or absent, thus the school might issue a detention: "Sorry, the problem is yours. Maybe tomorrow you will get dressed." If they remain home, they must stay in their room during normal school hours. No TV. No interactions with parents. Obviously, if both parents work an alternative plan is needed.

If the child is young and the school is cooperative, another plan can be developed with the help of the bus driver, the classroom teacher, and the principal. Tell the child the plan in advance. When it is time to leave for the bus, quietly take all of the clothes that have not yet been put on and place them in a bag. Wrap the child in a robe or coat and walk him or her to the bus, pajamas and all. The bus driver, having been briefed, smiles and says hello. The child gets on the bus with the bag of clothes. The parent then calls the principal to have the teacher alerted. If the child dresses on the bus, fine. If he or she arrives at school in pajamas, the teacher quietly says, "Would you like to go to the bathroom and get dressed?" The child will not starve without breakfast on this day, but he or she will have learned that dawdling no longer works. Only he or she is impacted on by the behavior.

This approach might work in other situations. At bedtime, whether in pajamas or still in street clothes, put the child in bed and turn out the lights. When the family is ready to leave for a movie, a visit, or a shopping trip and the child is not ready by the requested time, you should leave with the rest of the family. If the child cannot be left alone, have a sitter on call for the early phase of this approach so that you can follow through with the plan. Once the sitter is called, it is too late to change plans. Even if the child then quickly dresses, he or she still stays home. After a time or two, when he or she loses rather than the parents or the rest of the family, this child will get the message: "Finish your tasks on time or accept the consequences. You lose, not the rest of us."

❖   **Summary**

When a consistent behavioral plan is used in a family, unacceptable behaviors begin to change to more acceptable behaviors. Both parents regain control and confidence in their ability to parent. Children and adolescents learn that they can be controlled and that they will not be overwhelmed by not being in control. They are usually happier. Now, all of the positive experiences with the family reinforce the behaviors as well.

If the plan does not work or does not work as well as desired because of learning disabilities, a sensory integrative disorder, or other associated disorders or because the ADHD behaviors are not being managed by medication during all critical hours, these clinical issues must be addressed. The behavioral program should clarify these problems and help focus the needs.

If the plan does not work either because one or both parents do not follow the plan or defeat the plan or because the child or adolescent has such emotional problems that he or she cannot give up being in control or the need to be punished, more intensive individual, couples, or family therapy might be needed.

Chapter 13

Treatment With Medication

The use of medication to treat what is now called *attention-deficit hyperactivity disorder (ADHD)* was first described in 1937. During that year there was an epidemic of viral encephalitis. As they recovered from this disease, some of the children were observed to be hyperactive and distractible. Dr. C. Bradley, a pediatrician, tried a stimulant medication (Benzedrine) and found that the children became less active and distractible. Stimulants have been used to treat these behaviors ever since. It is important for you to understand that stimulant medications have been used to treat ADHD for over 50 years. Follow-up studies of patients with ADHD into adulthood show these medications to be effective and safe with no apparent long-term side effects.

Between 70% and 80% of children and adolescents with ADHD show improvement on the appropriate medication. These medications decrease or stop the hyperactivity, distractibility, and/or impulsivity, but they do not treat learning disabilities if they also exist. For some children and adolescents with ADHD manifested by hyperactivity, medication may result in improved motor control and possibly in improved handwriting. Individuals who are distractible might be better able to organize their thoughts when speaking or writing because of less interference with the thinking process. Short-term memory might improve because of a better ability to stay on task and concentrate. Likewise, individuals with impulsivity might perform better because they can now reflect before answering a question. For the same reason, they might be better able to use cognitive strategies for learning. However, the basic underlying psychological processes associated with the learning disabilities appear not to be changed.

There is no established protocol for treating ADHD with medication. In this chapter I present an approach that I find helpful. The protocol discussed should be seen as one possible model for thinking through each step of the clinical treatment process. Each clinician might use a variation of this model.

❖ Clinical Premises ❖

It is important that the necessary differential diagnostic process be considered before establishing the diagnosis of ADHD. If the clinician establishes this diagnosis, it is presumed that the behaviors are neurologically based. Therefore, because ADHD is not a school disability but a life disability, the need for medication must be assessed for each hour of each day. As stated earlier, to place a child or adolescent on medication only during school hours on school days will result in the individual doing better in school. However, he or she may continue to have difficulties within the family and in interactions with peers.

To take a child off of medication that is successfully treating ADHD and then send him or her to day camp or sleep-away camp over the summer is to invite problems. The concept of "drug holidays" started with the concern that the use of the stimulant medications might inhibit growth hormone and thus growth; therefore, the child needed to be off medication so that he or she could grow. This concern started after one study suggested such a possibility. Several major studies done since then have shown that growth hormone is released at night, when the child is off medication, and that there appears to be no concern with growth. Although the final answer is not yet known, the general view is that the clinician does not have to worry about growth problems. Once the appropriate medication is found, three important questions must be addressed:

1. How much medication is needed per dose?
2. How frequently is medication needed?
3. When should the person be on medication?

An approach to answering these questions is discussed below for each medication currently in use.

As noted before, there is nothing magical about puberty for children with ADHD. The only way to determine if they continue to need medication is to take them off the medication once or twice a year and observe whether the ADHD behaviors return. If they do, medication should be restarted. If they do not, the medications can be stopped.

❖ Clinical Protocol ❖

I find it helpful to have a format to follow in treating individuals with ADHD. In the absence of an established clinical protocol, I will discuss the one I use as a possible way to approach treatment. Treatment starts with one of the medications in what I call *Group I*. If these medications do not help or if the side effects create a problem that cannot be clinically resolved, *Group II* medications are tried. If these medications do not help or only help control some of the behaviors, a combination of Group I and Group II medications might be tried. If the patient still does not respond or if side effects require the clinician to try something else, *Group III* medications are considered.

Perhaps an analogy might help you understand the different medications. Picture a lake that does not have enough water in it. There are two ways to increase the level of water in the lake. One would be to pour in more water. (The stimulants increase the production of the needed neurotransmitter.) The other would be to build a dam, thus slowing down the outflow. In this way, the level will rise as well. (The tricyclic antidepressants slow down the breakdown process, thus allowing the neurotransmitter produced to stay around longer.)

Group I Medications

The medications in Group I are *stimulants* and are proposed to work by increasing the concentration of the deficient neurotransmitter norepinephrine at the nerve interface. They include

- Methylphenidate (Ritalin)
- Dextroamphetamine (Dexedrine)
- Pemoline (Cylert)

Group II Medications

The medications in Group II are called *tricyclic antidepressants*. They are proposed to work by inhibiting the uptake of norepinephrine, thus increasing the concentration of this transmitter at the nerve interface. They include

- Imipramine (Tofranil)
- Desipramine (Norpramin)

The tricyclic antidepressants may decrease the hyperactivity and distractibility. For reasons that are not clear, they might not be as helpful in decreasing the impulsivity. Thus if these medications help with some of the behaviors and not with the impulsivity, one of the Group I medications might be used in conjunction with the tricyclic antidepressant.

- Clonidine (Catapres) is not a tricyclic antidepressant; however, it may best be considered with the Group II medications.
- Bupropion (Wellbutrin) has been suggested as a medication for ADHD. Recent studies show it may be effective. It is not a tricyclic antidepressant; however, it does work at the nerve interface in a similar way.

Group III Medications

About 70% to 80% of children and adolescents with ADHD will respond to one of the medications in Group I or Group II or to a combination of these medications. However, 20% to 30% will be "nonresponders." Research to date does not clarify why these individuals do not respond to the medications. It is possible that the diagnosis is incorrect. Another possibility is that these individuals have another form of an attentional disorder. Another concept being considered is that for these individuals the presumed neurological problems are not in or not only in the reticular activating system. To use the symbolic model discussed in Chapter 10, perhaps the hyperactivity is not caused by a poorly functioning "brake" but by increased activity by the "accelerator" in the cortex. Possibly, distractibility is not caused by a poorly functioning "filter system" but by an oversensitive cortex. And, possibly, the impulsivity is not caused by a poorly functioning "circuit board" but by "short circuits" in the cortical areas (that is, perhaps the difficulties are not in the lower brain but in the cortical areas). Medications in Group III are presumed to "calm" the cortex. They include

- Thioridazine (Mellaril)
- Carbamazepine (Tegretol)

There is another small subgroup of persons in the "nonresponders" group who are now beginning to be clarified. There have been several case reports of young adults who were diagnosed as having ADHD when children and who responded well to the use of stimulant medication for years. However, each developed a *full bipolar disorder* (what used to be called *manic-depressive disorder*) in his or her early 20s. In these cases, there was a family history of bipolar illness. Also, the childhood descriptions included possible mood swings or changes in behavior. Because the characteristics in childhood for bipolar illness are not known, one must consider the possibility that, for some individuals, ADHD and bipolar disorders share a common neurochemical theme or that the behaviors of ADHD might be the earliest clinical evidence of this disorder. Such children and adolescents may respond very well to the use of lithium.

Some children or adolescents present with a complicated clinical picture suggesting multiple areas of brain dysfunction. They might show behaviors characteristic of individuals with pervasive developmental disorder. In addition, they might have learning disabilities and/or ADHD. These individuals might show some improvement with the Group I or Group II medications. When Group III medications are tried, some improvements may be found as well. It is possible that for this group both the cortex and the reticular activating system might be involved. Using this clinical lead, the use of a Group I or Group II medication along with a Group III medication may provide the best results.

It is presumed that medication was needed for both brain sites. To summarize, the medications in each of these groups are

- Group I medications
  - Methylphenidate (Ritalin)
  - Dextroamphetamine (Dexedrine)
  - Pemoline (Cylert)
- Group II medications
  - Imipramine (Tofranil)
  - Desipramine (Norpramin)
  - Clonidine (Catapres)
  - Bupropion (Wellbutrin)
- Group III medications
  - Thioridazine (Mellaril)
  - Carbamazepine (Tegretol)
  - Lithium

❖ Group I Medications: The Stimulants ❖

It is difficult to predict whether a child or adolescent with ADHD will respond better to one stimulant medication versus another. Some will respond poorly to one and have a positive response to another. Clinical findings, electroencephalograms (EEGs), and neurochemical measures do not appear to be useful predictors of stimulant responsiveness. The clinician must use his or her judgment as to which one to try first.

Each of these medications has shared and unique characteristics, effects, and side effects. Methylphenidate and dextroamphetamine are available in both short-acting and long-acting forms. Pemoline is only available in a long-acting form.

Methylphenidate (Ritalin) is available in 5-, 10-, and 20-milligram (mg) tablets and in a long-acting, Ritalin-SR tablet. Ritalin-SR contains 20 mg of methylphenidate and releases approximately 10 mg initially and 10 mg four hours later. Although there are references to the amount needed per kilogram of body weight, the amount needed by each individual does not seem to relate to body weight. A young child and an adult might need the same amount. The average dose is 15 mg to 30 mg per day in divided doses. Some individuals may require more. The Food and Drug Administration (FDA) guidelines recommend up to 60 mg per day; however, more may be used if clinically necessary and carefully monitored. If the medication is metabolized rapidly and only lasts about three hours, it may be necessary to give four or five doses a day, thus, in some cases, using more than 60 mg.

Dextroamphetamine (Dexedrine) is available in 5-mg tablets and in long-acting 5-, 10-, and 15-mg spansules. As with methylphenidate, the dose is established more by clinical observations than by the specific body weight. The FDA guidelines set the lower age limit at three years. The upper dose limit recommended is 40 mg per day; however, more can be used if clinically necessary.

Pemoline (Cylert) is available in 18.75-, 37.5-, and 75-mg tablets and in 37.5-mg chewable tablets. It is administered as a single oral dose each morning; though, an evening dose may be used. The recommended starting dose is 37.5 mg per day. The dose can be increased gradually by 18.75 mg each time. The maximum recommended daily dose is 112.5 mg; however, older adolescents and adults may need a higher dose.

Because methylphenidate is the most frequently used of the Group I medications, I will use it to discuss the clinical use of these Group I medications. Because you are most likely to hear this medication referred to by the trade name Ritalin, I will use this name. Remember that the generic name is methylphenidate.

Ritalin in the short-acting form begins to work in 30 to 45 minutes in most individuals. Recent studies show that it is not necessary to take the medication on an empty stomach. Food does not impair absorption of this medication; thus it can be given with a meal or after a meal. Each dose lasts between three and five hours. It appears that the amount needed per dose is a reflection of the speed with which the medication is absorbed and metabolized. The functional blood level may be the same for the individual who needs 5 mg, 10 mg, 15 mg, or 20 mg per dose.

Given these clinical factors, the three questions noted earlier have to be addressed by the clinician: 1) how much medication is needed per dose? 2) how often is the medication needed? and 3) during what time periods should the medication be used?

Because I strongly believe that parents must be informed, I will discuss more details on each medication than some may want. You must know what I expect each physician to know.

The initial medical workup should include measurements of height, weight, pulse, and blood pressure. The child or adolescent should be observed for tics and involuntary movements, and a history of tic disorders in the family should be obtained. If pemoline is to be used, liver function tests should be performed. No such tests are required for methylphenidate and dextroamphetamine. Medical follow-up at each visit should include observing for tics and involuntary movements. Measurements of pulse, blood pressure, weight, and height should be checked. If pemoline is used, liver function tests should be done every four to six months.

Establishing the Dose

The dose-response relationships vary widely among individuals. The best way to establish the dose needed is not by obtaining frequent blood levels but by clinical monitoring of therapeutic effects and side effects.

The usual starting dose is 5 mg each time taken. For a child under five years old, 2.5 mg might be considered. The dose can be increased by 2.5 mg or 5 mg per dose every two to three days until the maximum benefit is noted. I usually start each individual on a program of three times a day, seven days a week. Only in this way can the parents, the child or adolescent, the teachers, and I assess the benefits from the medication. Later (as is discussed below), the specific times of coverage can be determined.

Clinical judgment is used to establish the best dose. I start at the lowest dose I believe best and increase the dose by 2.5 mg or 5 mg until all persons involved report maximum benefit. At times, I might increase the dosage in steps to build in a model for observation. In other words, I might increase the morning dose but not the noon dose (for example, 10 mg at 8:00 A.M. and 5 mg at noon and at 4:00 P.M.). I then ask the teacher to observe whether the child or adolescent is better able to sit and attend in the morning compared with in the afternoon.

Feedback from teachers, as well as from parents, is critical in assessing the improvement in the hyperactivity, distractibility, and/or impulsivity. One efficient way for you to help the physician in this is to talk with the teacher at the end of each school day and then relay this information back to your physician. Thus one call to the physician can provide feedback from the school and home.

When determining the best dose to reach maximum benefit, it is useful to increase the dose until this point is reached. There are two side effects that suggest the dose is too high. If either occurs, the dose should be lowered. One side effect is emotional lability, which means the child or adolescent becomes upset more easily than usual, crying or having tantrums. The other side effect is that some children or adolescents appear to be "in a cloud" or "in a daze" or overfocused. They appear to be "spaced out," possibly described as "glassy-eyed."

I find it best to start with a short-acting form of the medication until the appropriate dose and time of dose is established. Then, a longer-acting form might be considered. If a child is started on Ritalin-SR first, the clinician cannot judge whether he or she might have needed less per dose. If 10 mg per dose is too high for this child, the use of the long-acting form might result in emotional lability or "spacey" behavior. Once the dose is established, the long-acting form can be considered if the amount needed for two consecutive doses equals the amount released in the long-acting form.

Establishing the Dose Interval

The average length of action for a short-acting tablet is four hours. However, for some individuals, the medication may last two-and-a-half to three hours; for others it may last up to five hours or more. Thus the dose interval must be established for each individual. There is nothing special about using Ritalin every four hours.

The dose interval is determined clinically, using the feedback from the parents, the teacher, and the child or adolescent. As an example, a boy is placed on Ritalin 5 mg at 8:00 A.M., noon, and 4:00 P.M. daily. If the feedback throughout the day is good, the dose interval may be best. If the teacher says, "You know, John is great in the morning. But, about 11:00 or 11:30 he begins to wiggle in his seat and can't stay on task. He is perfect again after he gets his noon medication." Perhaps, the dose interval for John is three hours. He may need his medication at 8:00 A.M., 11:00 A.M., and 2:00 P.M. A 5:00 P.M. dose might also be added.

If the teacher reports, "Alice is great in the morning. Only, between 12:30 and 1:00 she gets so upset. If I look at her the wrong way, she cries [Or, she seems to be in a cloud and cannot be reached.] By 1:00 or 1:30 she is fine again." Perhaps, for Alice the dose interval is five hours. The noon dose starts to work at about 12:30 to 12:45 P.M., before the morning dose has been metabolized. For a period of time, she is getting too much medication. Because the interval dose for her might be every five hours, she might take medication at 8:00 A.M., 1:00 P.M., and 6:00 P.M.

Sometimes parents report that their child or adolescent is significantly improved when on the medication, but there are still significant problems in the daily routine. For example, a girl is given her morning dose just before she leaves for school at 7:45 A.M. However, between the time she gets up and the time the medication starts to work, she is impossible. Because of the hyperactivity, distractibility, and/or impulsivity she has difficulty staying on task, getting dressed on time, and getting along with her siblings. The result is often a morning full of nagging, yelling, and fighting. In this situation, it would be ideal to provide the benefits of the medication during the early morning hours as well. The first dose may need to be given earlier and the following doses adjusted accordingly. For example, I might advise the parents to wake the child about 30 to 45 minutes before she has to get out of bed and give her the first dose. By the time she gets up, the medication is working, and the morning goes well for all. If this time is 6:30 A.M., the child may need to take the later doses at 10:30 A.M. and 2:30 P.M. A fourth dose may be needed at 6:30 P.M.

The same reasoning can be used for other problem situations. Suppose a boy gets the first dose at 8:00 A.M. as he leaves for school. There are problems on the school bus. He will not sit in the seat or gets into trouble with the other children. By the time school starts he is fine. The morning dose may have to be given earlier so that it is working by the time he gets on the bus. Or suppose a girl is given a third dose at 4:00 P.M. and it wears off by about 8:00 P.M. If she has behavioral difficulties

from 8:00 P.M. until bedtime at 9:30 or 10:00 P.M. (such as trouble getting ready for bed, following routines, and getting along with her siblings), it might be appropriate to consider a fourth dose at 8:00 P.M. to
help through these evening hours.

The basic principle to remember is that the medication lasts about
four hours. The clinician, the parents, and the child or adolescent need
to learn just how long the medication lasts for this individual and then
look at units of time to assess if the ADHD behaviors are interfering
with functioning. If the behaviors are interfering, medication coverage
for these hours may be indicated. The model of giving the medication
at 8:00 A.M., noon, and 4:00 P.M. needs to be individualized for each
child or adolescent.

Establishing the Periods of Time to Be Covered

Because ADHD is a neurologically based disorder, the child or adolescent will be hyperactive, distractible, and/or impulsive throughout his
or her hours awake. It is important to clinically assess each individual
in his or her total environment to determine during which hours medication coverage is needed. There are no confirmed contraindications
to the use of these medications on a continuous basis. Further, clinical
research has shown that the amount of the medication in the blood at
any one time is the same for individuals who take the medication on a
chronic basis as it is for the individual who takes a single dose. Thus
medication can be programmed around three-, four-, or five-hour units
of time without concern that time is needed to accumulate the appropriate blood level or that such treatment will make the child or adolescent worse.

The key is to observe the effect of the ADHD behaviors. Hyperactivity, distractibility, and/or impulsivity can be a problem whenever
such behaviors interfere with what is expected. Each behavior may interfere with functioning in the classroom or in any school-like activity
such as religious education, Sunday School, or homework. These behaviors might interfere with scout meetings or related activities. Some
children or adolescents (or their coaches) note that they can concentrate and play sports better when they are on the medication.

The impact of some of these behaviors will depend on the age, grade, school demand, and family style. For example, a first or second grader might have no or little homework. Thus if he or she is distractible, medication will be needed during school hours but may not be needed during after-school hours. However, this same child might need medication during these hours, when he or she becomes older and has more homework. Likewise, a hyperactive child might need medication during school hours, but if he or she is young and spends most of the after-school hours playing outside and if the family does not mind the fidgetiness, medication may not be needed at home. Again, because of increases in homework or family demands, the same child might need medication for these hours when older.

Weekends and holidays must be thought through in the same way. If the ADHD behaviors interfere with expected activities or performance, medication will be needed. For example, suppose the family of a hyperactive eight-year-old boy plans a weekend trip. They will drive for four hours to get to the grandparents. Once there, the boy will run around and play with his cousins for most of the time. Finally, there will be the four-hour ride home. He might need medication coverage during each four-hour car ride and during the quiet family dinners; however, he might not need medication during the remainder of the weekend.

In determining which hours must be covered, I try to educate the parents and the child on how the medication works. If they know that it starts to work in about 30 to 45 minutes, that it lasts between three and five hours, and that while on the medication the child has a decrease in ADHD behaviors, they can think through units of time with the clinician and decide when medication is needed. Often the child or adolescent will be the best clinician. One child recently asked me if he could use the medication when he played soccer. He told me, "I can concentrate on the game so much better when I am on the medicine."

Using Long-Acting Medications

Once the dose, time of dose, and time of coverage is determined, the clinician can consider using a long-acting form of the medication. For Ritalin, the long-acting form can be considered only if 10 mg is needed for each of two successive doses. Recent studies suggest that for some individuals the Ritalin-SR appears to take longer to begin to show an effect and to only last four to five hours. Thus it may not work as well as taking two individual 10-mg doses four hours apart. If the Ritalin-SR tablet is chewed or cut in half instead of swallowed whole, the blood level is unpredictable and the child or adolescent might show evidence of too high a dose for part of the time and of too low a dose for other times.

For dextroamphetamine, the options for a long-acting form are greater because there are 5-mg, 10-mg, and 15-mg spansules available, each lasting about eight hours.

Pemoline only comes in a long-acting form. The amount taken each morning must be determined. Because the medication must be used each day to maintain the proper level, the time of coverage is not an issue.

Side Effects and Their Management

To review the side effects most often seen with Group I medications and how they might be managed, I will again use Ritalin as an example. Later, I will note the less frequent side effects listed in the pharmaceutical literature.

The two side effects of Ritalin most frequently found are loss of appetite and difficulty falling asleep at night. Of much less frequent occurrence, some individuals will complain of a stomachache or headache. Of even less frequent occurrence, tics may develop with some children or adolescents. As noted above, there are two side effects that suggest the dose of medication may be too high for an individual: emotional lability and a confused, cloudy cognitive state.

Loss of appetite. Ritalin may decrease an individual's appetite. This side effect may decrease over the first several weeks and cease to be a problem. If it persists, something must be done. The first step is to observe eating patterns. The medication may take the edge off of the appetite; thus the child might not finish his or her meals but may eat candy, cake, and other sweets. If this is true, parents need to limit such sweets unless the meal is eaten. Some children are not hungry and do not eat their lunch at school. They return home at about 3:30 P.M. as the noon dose wears off and are hungry. They eat a huge snack and then cannot eat dinner. Parents need to offer smaller or lower-calorie snacks after school.

In some cases, none of the above approaches work, and the child continues to eat less than before starting the medication. He or she may lose weight or not gain weight. The next step is to try to create "windows of opportunity." I try to give the first dose after breakfast if at all possible. Because the child will have been off the medication overnight, he or she should have a normal appetite and eat well. I accept that lunch will not be great. Parents might try to make a meal the child is more likely to want, such as a jelly sandwich rather than a tuna fish sandwich. Teachers should be alerted that the child may not eat lunch and that this is alright. For some children, this free time might mean the need for more supervision during lunch. Rather than give the third dose at 4:00 P.M., I try to hold off until dinner time or around 5:30 to 6:00 P.M. In this way, there might be a period of time off of medication when the appetite might return. The child might need more structure and supervision during the time off of medication. Homework might be delayed until later. If none of these approaches work, a Group II medication might have to be considered.

Sleep difficulties. Some children and adolescents have difficulty going to sleep when they take Ritalin. This problem often lessens or goes away over the first two to three weeks. If it does not, an intervention is needed. For some children, it is the medication that keeps them awake; for others, it is the lack of medication that keeps them awake. Each possibility must be explored. Each reason leads to a different management approach.

If it is the medication that results in difficulty falling asleep and if the problem occurs only occasionally, your physician might recommend diphenhydramine (Benadryl). A dose of 25 mg to 50 mg at bedtime might help the child or adolescent fall asleep. It is important for the child to know that the medication is not a sleeping pill. They cannot read or play until they get sleepy. However, if they lie quietly in the dark and try to sleep, the medication may help them fall asleep. This medication might help the child or adolescent return to a pattern of sleeping and then be phased out. For some, it might be needed occasionally. It is best not to use it every night on a regular basis. If the sleep problems persist, the 4:00 P.M. dose of the Group I medication may have to be decreased or stopped. If this change creates behavioral problems in the afternoon and evening or when doing homework, a Group II medication might have to be considered.

For other individuals, a lack of medication might cause sleep problems. If a child takes the medication three times a day, he or she is functioning "normally" from about 8:00 A.M. to about 8:00 P.M. (that is, he or she is no longer hyperactive, distractible, and/or impulsive). The medication wears off, and the behaviors return, sometimes with greater intensity. The child is not used to being this way and cannot lie still, block out stimuli, and fall asleep. For these individuals, a fourth dose of medication at about 8:00 P.M., allowing for the decrease or stopping of the ADHD behaviors may allow them to fall asleep with no difficulty.

I know of no way to distinguish which of the above reasons cause the sleep problem. I advise parents and the child or adolescent of the possibilities and ask them to help decide which is causing the problem. I ask that they pick an evening when staying up very late will not be a disaster, maybe a Friday or Saturday. I have the individual take a fourth dose of the medication at 8:00 P.M. If the medication is causing the sleep problem, he or she will have great difficulty going to sleep. I advise the family that if this happens, Benedryl can be used. If the added evening dose of the medication results in the individual going to sleep with no difficulty, I have learned that it is the lack of medication that is causing the problem. This fourth dose might be used every day.

Stomachache.   The reason for this side effect is not known. It is my suspicion that the cause relates to the fact that the stimulant medications decrease gastrointestinal motility, resulting in food remaining in the stomach longer. I have tried a high-fiber diet based on this possibility with no success. I know of no approach that corrects this side effect. If it persists, a Group II medication may be needed.

Headache.   The reason for this side effect is also not known. If the headaches persist, it will be necessary to try a Group II medication.

Tics.   Tics might begin immediately or months after the medication is started. The most common tics are of the head or neck muscles. Some will involve the pharyngeal muscles (those in the back of the throat), resulting in sniffing, snorting, or coughing. Once the tics begin, I prefer to stop the medication and to change to a Group II medication. Sometimes it takes up to six months for the tics to stop completely. If there is a family history of a muscle tic disorder or of Tourette syndrome, there is an increased concern that the stimulant medication might initiate this disorder earlier than it might have been genetically set to start and that stopping the medication will not result in the tics going away. If such a tic disorder already exists, there is the concern that the stimulant medication might aggravate the disorder. Thus it is important to explore if there is a family history of a tic disorder before starting a Group I medication and, if there is, to inform the physician. There are two views in medicine at this time. One group believes that if there is a history of a tic disorder, Ritalin should be used and if tics develop they should be treated. The other group believes that if there is a history of a motor tic disorder or Tourette syndrome or if the child or adolescent has been diagnosed as having such a disorder, the ADHD should not be treated with a stimulant medication. Each clinician must decide what to do. My preference is to use a Group II medication or other medication if there is any concern about a tic disorder.

Emotional lability and cloudy cognitive ability.   As mentioned above, these two behaviors suggest that the dose of the medication is too high for the individual. The reason for these behaviors is not known. These side effects stop once the dose has been lowered to the appropriate level.

Height growth impairment.   I discussed this problem earlier, but because many parents worry about it, I will mention it again. Research does not support the earlier fear that the stimulant medications inhibit growth. The few studies that suggest this to be true show that slowing of height gain rarely reaches clinical significance. It is important to understand that even these studies show that height loss, if it occurs, may be only one to three centimeters (less than one inch).

My clinical understanding of the data leads me to use the medication without concern about height. I do not feel there is a need for vacations off medication nor for the need to stop the use of these medications before age 15.

Other side effects. The pharmaceutical literature describes other cardiovascular, central nervous system, gastrointestinal, allergic, and endocrine difficulties. These are extremely uncommon. The clinician should be familiar with these possibilities, inform you of them, and watch for them. Unlike the other stimulant medications, pemoline can impact on liver function. Thus, as noted earlier, periodic liver function tests should be done.

Other Clinical Issues

Preschool children. When stimulant medications are used with preschool children, there may be a higher frequency of side effects, especially emotional lability, manifested by sadness or irritability. It is possible that these side effects are secondary to the children's sensitivity to the medication and to the need for lower doses.

Tolerance. No research data have shown the appearance of tolerance to stimulant medications over time, with the possible exception of Ritalin-SR.

Rebound. Some children and adolescents seem to experience a rebound effect when the Ritalin is metabolized and the blood level drops. They not only return to their previous level of hyperactivity, distractibility, and/or impulsivity, but may be excitable, talkative, impulsive, or have insomnia. This rebound behavior might last for an hour or more. Often, the problem lessens or stops after several weeks on the medication. If the rebound does not stop, the last dose of the day might need to be decreased. If this change creates a problem, one might try to add a fourth dose to see if the evening can be handled without the rebound and the child can go to sleep before the dose wears off. If none of these approaches work, a change to a Group II medication might be needed.

Impact of other medications. The pharmaceutical literature covers this topic in great detail. Your physician will monitor for any possible problems. Here I discuss the more common medications only.

For some children or adolescents, the additional use of a decongestant medication might increase the hyperactivity or make them feel agitated. The use of theophylline (a medication often used for asthma) might cause the same reaction. In each case, if the new medication must be continued over a long period of time, a change to a Group II medication might be considered. If the new medication is to be used for a short period of time, the amount of Ritalin might be increased for this time.

Some sedatives and antihistamines appear to decrease the effectiveness of Ritalin. When taking both, some individuals appear to have "broken away" from the medication; their ADHD behaviors return. It may be necessary to increase the dose during the time these other medications are used, returning to the appropriate dose after they are stopped. This problem might occur when a child on Ritalin gets a cold and is placed on an antihistamine. He or she becomes more hyperactive, distractible, and/or impulsive. The physician concludes that the child is older and may need more medication. With an increase in dose, the behaviors improve. However, once the cold improves and the antihistamine is stopped, the child might become emotionally labile or appear to be in a cloud. Not knowing why this happened, the physician might stop all medication to "reassess," and the child begins to have problems at school and home.

Another situation might occur before surgery. Certain sedatives appear to cause ADHD behaviors to become worse. If a child is taken off Ritalin before surgery and given a preanesthetic (usually a short-acting sedative, such as a barbiturate), rather than calming down and getting sleepy, he or she becomes more active. More barbiturate may be given, and the child becomes even more active.

Fever. For reasons that are not yet understood, when children with ADHD have a fever they often become calm and mellow. The ADHD behaviors seem to lessen or stop. Some parents report that they love it when their child has a fever because he or she will cuddle in their lap and be so calm. It is unclear at this time if children on Ritalin should go off of the medication during the period of the fever. I usually advise that they do and find that the behaviors remain under control.

Other Information

In the earlier literature, some professionals raised the question of "state-dependent" learning: If a child learns something while on a medication, will he or she retain this information when off of the medication? Studies show no such problem with any of the Group I medications.

Because the dose does not appear to be related to weight, children and adolescents on a Group I medication usually do not need a higher dose as they grow in size or height. Many may need the same dose over many years.

At one time the use of a Group I medication with a child or adolescent with a seizure disorder was considered unwise. At this time this concern appears no longer to be an issue. Children and adolescents with a seizure disorder should be evaluated on an individual basis; however, the use of a Group I medication can be considered.

The question of addiction is noted in the pharmaceutical literature. Reference is made to the possibility of abuse. At the low doses used, addiction has not been reported to be an issue. Current studies suggest that dextroamphetamine probably carries a higher risk than Ritalin and that pemoline probably carries relatively less risk. For those children or adolescents with ADHD who also have a conduct disorder, special supervision may be needed to observe whether the medications are being sold to peers. There is no evidence that substance abuse is increased by the use of stimulant medications. You should be advised of the concerns but assured that under proper management addiction is not likely to occur.

❖ **Group II Medications:** ❖
The Tricyclic Antidepressants

Group II medications are used if the Group I medications do not work or if they produce side effects that cannot be clinically managed. Another indication might be an attempt to obtain a smoother, even effect from medication when a Group I medication does not last long or there is a rebound effect. Both imipramine and desipramine are long acting; thus the time for each dose and the time period covered by the medication are not issues.

Imipramine

Imipramine is available in 10-, 25-, and 50-mg tablets. The FDA guidelines suggest use for children six years old or older. There is no apparent relationship between plasma level and clinical improvement. A starting dose for children might be 10 mg in the morning and 10 mg at bedtime. Unlike with Group I medications, it might take three to five days before the benefits of imipramine can be assessed. The dose can be increased every three to five days until the maximum benefit is reached. Usually, the additional dose can be added in the evening or in the morning. If the feedback suggests that the child or adolescent is not doing as well during the middle of the day, the total dose can be divided into three parts and taken in the morning, early afternoon (thus avoiding the need to give the medication at school), and evening.

Imipramine works best in decreasing hyperactivity and distractibility. My clinical experience shows it to have less of an effect on impulsivity. If impulsivity persists, a small amount of a Group I medication might be added. Often, because both Group I and Group II medications produce a relative increase in the suspected neurotransmitter at the nerve interface, less is needed of each when used together. If a Group I medication was stopped because of side effects, the lower dose needed in conjunction with a Group II medication may not result in the side effect.

Imipramine may produce electroencephalographic (EEG) changes at doses higher than the recommended level. It should not be used if the child or adolescent has a seizure disorder because it might lower the threshold for seizures. It cannot be used if the child is on a particular antidepressant called a monoamine oxidase inhibitor (MAOI). Further, adolescents must be warned that imipramine may enhance the nervous system depressant effects of alcohol.

The primary clinical side effect of imipramine is sedation (sleepiness). If the child or adolescent complains of being tired or is observed to fall asleep in class, the dose may have to be lowered, given in divided doses over the day, or given primarily at bedtime. Other clinical side effects might be a dry mouth or constipation. Although very uncommon, imipramine can impact on blood cell production, primarily causing a decrease in a particular blood cell called a neutrophil, and can impact on liver function. Thus a differential blood count and a liver function battery should be done initially and every four to six months thereafter while the medication is being used. If changes are noted, the medication should be discontinued.

Tricyclic antidepressants can cause heart blockage or irregular heart rhythms. There might be specific electrocardiographic (ECG) changes. These effects appear to be dose related and uncommon in children and adolescents. Most deaths associated with these drugs have been with adults and have occurred after deliberate or accidental overdose or in patients with preexisting abnormalities in cardiac conduction. To detect a preexisting cardiac conduction defect, a baseline ECG is recommended. Follow-up ECGs should be part of follow-up care.

Desipramine

Desipramine is a metabolite of imipramine. It is available in 10-, 25-, 50-, 75-, 100-, and 150-mg tablets. At this time the pharmaceutical literature does not recommend its use for children. It is not listed as a treatment for ADHD. However, studies show that it can be effective for ADHD.

The contraindications and side effects for desipramine are the same as those for imipramine. Three cases have been reported of a child having a sudden death while being treated with desipramine. With one eight-year-old boy, there had been no known cardiac abnormalities. He had been on the medication for two years as a treatment for ADHD. Plasma levels of desipramine obtained from all three of these children were in the therapeutic or subtherapeutic range. Although there was no clear link, the studies suggested possible cardiac toxicity. Perhaps you have read about these children.

The currently available information about these sudden deaths is limited but suggests that the children were not receiving unusually high doses of desipramine nor were their blood levels reported to be above the therapeutic range at the time they were obtained. In each case, the cardiac status of these children before the event was not known. Thus there is no way to show that desipramine caused a direct toxic effect that led to sudden death in healthy children.

It is possible that the children had preexisting but undetected cardiac conduction defects (that is, the electrical activity that paces the heart beat was not functioning properly) or structural anomalies and that their deaths were completely unrelated to exposure to desipramine. It is also possible that desipramine exacerbated a preexisting, undetected cardiac conduction defect or structural anomaly. Or perhaps desipramine had unusual effects on an immature cardiac conduction system. There are no data to support any of these possibilities.

The current literature suggests increased caution in the use of desipramine and, possibly, other tricyclic drugs in the treatment of prepubertal children. Although the limited information available does not provide an adequate basis for developing an informed recommendation, it is suggested that an ECG be obtained at baseline and during medication "loading" and steady state. It may be contraindicated to administer tricyclic antidepressants to children who have suggestions of conduction problems. A more comprehensive evaluation may be needed for children with a positive family history of cardiac conduction defects or sudden death. My preference at this time is not to use desipramine with children and adolescents.

Clonidine

If the use of a Group I medication results in minimal improvement or in side effects that cannot be controlled, the use of clonidine might be considered. Clonidine appears to be helpful in treating hyperactivity or aggressiveness but may not significantly improve distractibility. This medication appears to improve frustration tolerance and compliance with children and adolescents who also have an oppositional defiant or conduct disorder. Clonidine comes in 0.1-, 0.2-, and 0.3-mg tablets and in a transdermal therapeutic system (TTS patch). The patch comes in different strengths programmed to deliver either 0.1, 0.2, or 0.3 mg of clonidine per day for one week.

The usual dose is 0.15 mg to 0.3 mg per day. The medication is given in divided doses three to four times a day with meals and at bedtime. The usual starting dose is one-fourth to one-half of the 0.1-mg tablet (0.024 mg to 0.05 mg) given in the evening. The dose can be increased by adding a similar dose in the morning. If needed, a third similar dose might be added in the morning. Clonidine is a short-acting medication; thus such frequent doses may be necessary. Once the best dose is established with oral medications, the use of the patch might be considered. It might take several months to observe benefits from the medication.

The patch provides slow absorption through the skin and avoids the marked changes in blood levels that occur when using the tablets. It is suggested that one-fourth to one-half of a Catapres-TTS patch be used.

The most frequent side effect of clonidine is sedation, usually seen during the day. This sleepiness is most likely to occur during the first two to four weeks and then often decreases. As an antihypertensive agent, clonidine may produce hypotension (a drop in blood pressure). In children, a 10% decrease in systolic pressure may be detected, but this change generally produces no clinical symptoms or discomfort. The patch might produce an allergic skin reaction and have to be discontinued.

The initial medical workup should include a recording of blood pressure and pulse. Blood pressure and pulse should be obtained weekly during the first month of clonidine treatment. Once the dose is stabilized, these measurements can be obtained every two months. Information on sedation should be obtained on a regular basis.

If clonidine appears to work but some behaviors remain and the clinician is hesitant to increase the dose, methylphenidate or dextroamphetamine might be added. The two in combination might produce better results.

Bupropion

As noted earlier, bupropion has been suggested for use when all other Group I and Group II medications are not effective. The research on the use of this medication is new, and much of it has not yet been published. If your physician uses this medication she or he will review the details with you.

❖   **Group III Medications**   ❖

Each of the medications in Group III is very different and must be discussed separately. Often the amount of medication that is needed is less than would be used for the primary clinical disorders usually treated by these medications. Because each is different, it is necessary for the clinician to review the pharmaceutical literature in detail with the parents.

Thioridazine

Thioridazine comes in 10-, 15-, 25-, 50-, 100-, 150-, and 200-mg tablets, as well as in a concentrate form of 30 mg or 100 mg strength and in a 25-mg and 100-mg suspension. The FDA guidelines approve the use of this medication starting at age two. It is approved for ADHD. The starting dose can be as low as 10 mg in the morning and 10 mg at bedtime. The effect of the medication might not be noticed for three to five days. The dose can be increased by 10 mg each three to five days until maximum benefit is noted. If the child or adolescent does not do as well during midday, the dosage can be given in three divided amounts over the day.

The main side effect of thioridazine is sedation. If present, the dose may have to be decreased, given in divided doses, or given primarily at bedtime. Another possible side effect—a specific muscle problem called *tardive dyskinesia*—is not common at the low doses used for ADHD, but clinicians must look for it. Individuals with tardive dyskinesia appear not to be able to move the muscles of their face and cannot make facial expressions. Other side effects include dryness of mouth and nasal stuffiness. Finally, the child taking thioridazine might be more sensitive to sunlight and need more sunscreen protection.

A rare few individuals taking thioridazine may show motor restlessness. This is sometimes difficult to distinguish from certain forms of hyperactivity in children and can be confused with a worsening of symptoms or agitation. This clinical condition is characterized by pacing, restless feelings in the legs, a central state of agitation, dysphoria or irritability, and an inability to sit still. It is uncommon with children. Parkinsonian symptoms such as muscular rigidity, finger and hand tremor, drooling, akinesia, and masklike faces are rare in children.

There are no specific laboratory tests needed prior to the use of this medication. During follow-up visits no specific studies are needed. Careful observations for the presence of abnormal movements should be made.

Carbamazepine

Carbamazepine is available in 100- and 200-mg tablets. A starting dose of 100 mg at bedtime is recommended. For children under age 12, the dose can be increased by 100 mg given in the morning and at bedtime for a recommended maximum dose of 1,000 mg. For individuals over 12, a maximum dose of 1,200 mg can be considered. The dose needed for ADHD is usually less than that needed for control of a seizure disorder.

It is important to monitor the blood level to maintain a therapeutic level and to avoid a toxic level. The more common side effects of carbamazepine are dizziness, drowsiness, nausea, and vomiting. Because of possible side effects impacting on the blood or cardiovascular system or on liver function, careful monitoring is needed. More details on side effects should be provided by the physician.

Lithium

Lithium carbonate comes in 300-mg capsules and 300-mg tablets, as well as in 450-mg controlled release tablets. The amount needed will vary with each individual. The goal is to reach a therapeutic range in the blood.

Side effects of lithium might include hand tremor, frequent urination, and mild thirst. Transient and mild nausea and general discomfort may be seen. These side effects may decrease over time. More details on side effects should be provided by the physician.

❖ **Summary** ❖

Medication to treat ADHD must be seen as part of a multimodal approach that includes education, counseling, behavioral management, and working closely with the school. If any of the associated disorders are present, they must be treated as well.

If your son or daughter has ADHD and medication is needed, you must work closely with your physician. The information provided in this chapter is meant to help you be informed so that you know what is being done and why. If you find that you now know more than your family doctor, find a way of lending him or her a copy of this chapter. If he or she does not believe in medication or refuses to work with you on establishing dose or handling side effects (saying "Give him [or her] these pills and come back in a month"), consider another physician.

Chapter 14

Other Nonmedication Treatments for ADHD

Two areas of clinical observation suggest possible themes relating to attention-deficit hyperactivity disorder (ADHD). These observations have lead to proposed nonmedication treatments. None have been successful; however, efforts in these areas continue. One observation is that there is a relationship between nutrition and behavior. No clear patterns or interventions have been clarified, but the relationship is apparent. The other observation is that there is a relationship between allergies and behavior. It is hoped that future research will add to the understanding of these relationships, especially the relationship food and allergies may have with ADHD. In this chapter, I review what is known or proposed for now.

❖ ## Nutrition and Behavior ❖

The first major effort to relate a nutritional issue to ADHD was proposed by Dr. Benjamin Feingold. His concepts and the research on this theory and therapy are discussed first. Other professionals have proposed other nutritional concepts. These are reviewed below.

Food Additives and Preservatives

In his 1975 book, *Why Your Child Is Hyperactive,* Dr. Feingold pro-posed that synthetic flavors and colors in the diet were related to hy-peractivity. He reported that the elimination of all foods containing artificial colors and flavors as well as salicylates and certain other addi-tives would stop the hyperactivity. Neither in this book nor in any of his other publications did Dr. Feingold present research data to con-firm his theory or the success of the treatment. All findings were based on his clinical experience. He and his book received wide publicity. It was left to others to document whether he was correct or incorrect. Because of a hope that he might be correct and a need either to counter his claims or to prove he was correct, the federal government funded several research centers to do research in this area. Basically, two different types of clinical studies were done: dietary-crossover de-signs and specific-challenge designs.

Dietary-crossover studies. In the dietary-crossover studies, hyper-active children were randomly assigned either to the elimination diet or to a control diet and then crossed over to the other treatment. The researchers found ambiguous results. In one study, improvement in behavior was noted in a few children but only by the teachers of those who were given the control diet first (followed by the elimination diet). The findings were not noted when the order was reversed. In another study, the parents noted improvement with the elimination diet; how-ever, the objective measures of hyperactivity showed no improvement. These studies suggested that there may be a subset of hyperactive chil-dren, particularly younger children, who respond to some aspect of the elimination diet, but either such a group is extremely small or the effectiveness of the diet is much less dramatic and predictable than had been described in previous anecdotal reports.

Specific-challenge studies. The dietary-crossover studies showed that a different research approach was needed. The strategy was changed from testing the general efficacy of the overall elimination diet to considering the specific involvement of the artificial colors or flavors with the hyperactivity. In this specific-challenge design, the children were maintained on Feingold's elimination diet throughout the study. Periodically, the children were given (challenged with) foods that contained the suspected offending chemical (such as artificial food colors). Measures were taken to note if the hyperactive state was precipitated or aggravated by this challenge.

The data from these studies suggest that there does appear to be a subset of children with behavioral disturbances who respond to some aspects of the Feingold diet. However, as noted above, the controlled clinical studies indicate that this group is small. Further, with notable exceptions, the specific elimination of synthetic food colors from the diet did not appear to be a major factor in the reported responses of a majority of these children.

Research conclusions. In 1982 the National Institutes of Health held a Consensus Development Conference on Defined Diets and Childhood Hyperactivity. This conference was sponsored by the National Institute of Child Health and Human Development. A panel of experts reviewed all of the existing research and listened to reports and testimony from people who wanted to present to the group. They reached conclusions similar to those presented above. Specifically, they reported that "these studies did indicate a limited positive association between the 'defined diets' [that is, Feingold's diet] and a decrease in hyperactivity." The panel noted that there was insufficient evidence available to permit identification beforehand of this small group of individuals who may respond and to determine under what circumstances they may derive benefits. The panel members noted that the defined diets should not be used universally in the treatment of childhood hyperactivity at this time.

Two later literature reviews reached the same conclusions. The Feingold diet is not effective in treating hyperactivity in most children. There may be a small percentage, 1% to 2%, who appear to respond positively to the diet for reasons that are not yet clear. There is no way for the clinician to identify in advance which individuals might be part of this small group.

In clinical practice one observes some children with ADHD who become more active when they take medications (such as penicillin) with red or yellow dyes or when they have a large amount of foods with these dyes (such as cereals and drinks). It is possible that this small percentage of children are the ones who might benefit from the elimination diet.

Some studies in the recent literature present data that, according to the authors, support the therapeutic success of the Feingold diet. The final answers are not in; however, the preponderance of studies support the views of the Consensus Conference.

Refined Sugars

Clinical observations and parent reports suggest that refined sugars might promote adverse behavioral reactions in children.[1] These observations are not supported by clinical observations or studies. One research team studied the relationship between sugar intake and conduct disorders, learning disorders, and ADHD in children. Behavioral and classroom measures were made after intake of sucrose (a refined sugar), fructose (a natural sugar), and a placebo. The results did not distinguish the normal effects of increased energy intake from sugar effects, per se. Hence the investigators could not conclude that deviant behavior was increased by sugar.

Another sugar-challenge study reached the same conclusions. Knowing that some parents have reported an increase in activity level when their children ate a high-sugar snack or meal, the investigator placed an ad in a local newspaper seeking children diagnosed as having ADHD with such an observed adverse reaction to sugar. Children were accepted into the study if they had ADHD and if the parents claimed an immediate effect of sugar on their children's behavior following smaller amounts of sugar than were to be given in the challenge study. There was no significant effect of glucose, fructose, or

---

[1] Two theories have been proposed for this possible reaction. One is that certain sugars (such as glucose) could influence brain neurotransmitter levels and, thus, the activity level in hyperactive children. The other concept is that carbohydrate intake influences the level of fatty acids essential for the synthesis of prostaglandin in the brain. Insulin is required in this critical step to activate the prostaglandin precursors. Thus the level of essential fatty acids could be influenced by carbohydrate intake and could secondarily influence insulin production.

placebo on any of the behavioral measures either when the individual sugars were compared with placebo or when both sugars were combined. None of the behavioral challenges reported by the parents were observed.

Another researcher questioned whether the effects the parents reported might be based on the blood glucose level and not on the intake of sugar. He designed a study in which children were given one of three breakfasts. One was high in carbohydrates, especially refined sugars; one was high in protein; and one was high in fats. After these meals, each child was challenged with fructose, glucose, or placebo. The researcher found that those children reported by their parents as reacting to sugar intake with an increase in hyperactivity did show an increase in activity level if they were challenged with glucose after eating a high-carbohydrate meal.

It may be possible that refined sugars do increase the activity level of some hyperactive children if the blood sugar level is high enough. When the children's blood carbohydrate levels were high because of a high-carbohydrate breakfast and the children were then challenged with refined sugars, their activity levels went up. Possibly, it is the amount of refined sugar eaten over a brief period of time that results in this behavior.

Artificial Sweeteners

A recent study on aspartame (used in Equal and NutraSweet) suggests that some children with ADHD become more aggressive and noncompliant when given large doses of this artificial sweetener. However, no other information about this is currently available.

❖ ADHD and Allergies ❖

Pediatricians and pediatric allergists have reported for many years that a higher percentage of children with allergies have learning disabilities and/or ADHD than do children in the general population. Most studies in this research area have been done on the possible relationships between allergies and learning disabilities. Dr. Benjamin Feingold, a pediatric allergist, focused on ADHD. No studies to date have shown how allergies and these disorders relate. No treatment approaches have been confirmed to be successful.

Two clinicians have written about specific issues relating allergies to learning disabilities and/or ADHD and on specific treatment programs. Neither has presented research data that have been replicated by others. Hence, their proposed clinical findings and treatment approaches are not accepted in general by the medical community. However, because you might read books written by these clinicians, I review their concepts and treatment approaches here briefly.

Dr. Doris Rapp

Dr. Rapp believes that there is a relationship between food or other sensitivities and hyperactivity. She has proposed a diet that eliminates the identified foods or the avoidance of other suspected allergens as a treatment for hyperactivity. She believes that the traditional allergy skin testing for foods does not always detect the foods that cause problems. Her critics say that her sublingual challenge tests (that is, certain allergens placed under the tongue) are not valid measures of allergies.

Dr. Rapp has identified certain foods or food groups that children might be allergic to: milk, chocolate, eggs, wheat, corn, peanuts, pork, and sugar. She suggests that parents try a specific elimination diet described in her books. This diet consists of eliminating all of the possible allergy-producing foods and then adding one back each week to see if there is a change in behaviors. She uses a food extract solution placed under the tongue in her tests. If the child is found to be sensitive to certain foods or to certain chemicals in the environment (such as paste, glue, paint, mold, and chemicals found in new carpets), these items are eliminated or avoided. She reports an improvement in the behaviors of the child. Most specifically, she reports less aggressive or oppositional behavior and less hyperactivity.

If one reads Dr. Rapp's literature or reviews the videotapes of her testing children, one is impressed. On tape, a child is happily in his or her parents lap and interacting. A food extract solution of something the child has been found to be allergic to is placed under the tongue, and within a minute he or she becomes belligerent and very active. However, other clinicians and researchers have challenged her clinical reports and findings, noting that they do not get the same responses to the challenges nor the same benefits from the treatment. Thus her work is considered controversial.

I do not know what to believe at this time. I have seen patients who were evaluated by Dr. Rapp and placed on specific elimination diets or monitored to eliminate exposure to certain chemicals who improved (that is, their level of hyperactivity and aggressive behaviors decreased). On several occasions, exposure to the food or chemical resulted in several hours of hyperactivity and aggressive behavior. For some of these children, my clinical observations showed that a stimulant medication helped the ADHD; however, when the children were exposed to the suspected food or chemical, their hyperactivity increased. The final answers are not yet in.

Dr. William Crook

Dr. Crook has written extensively on the relationship between allergies and general health, learning disabilities, and ADHD. He writes of the "allergic-tension-fatigue syndrome." He also reports that specific allergies can result in hyperactivity and distractibility. Many of his more recent publications and presentations focus on the possible allergic reaction to a specific yeast and to the development of specific behaviors after a yeast infection. He reports that treatment of the yeast infection improves or corrects the problem. No clinical or research studies have confirmed Dr. Crook's theories or replicated his reported clinical success. Here, too, the final answers are not in.

❖ **Summary** ❖

There is a relationship between brain function and nutrition as well as between brain function and allergic reactions. Clinically, these relationships appear to be as true for ADHD as for other brain disorders. Although research activity in these areas has increased, no consistent findings have been established.

There will continue to be proposed treatments based on these relationships. It is hoped that future research and clinical findings will clarify these relationships and will lead to better treatments for ADHD.

Adults

Chapter 15

Adults With ADHD

The exact percentage of children with attention-deficit hyperactivity disorder (ADHD) who continue to have this disorder as adults is not yet known. As noted throughout this book, studies suggest that about 50% of children with ADHD will continue to have the disorder as adolescents. Of these adolescents, 50% (that is, about 25% of children with ADHD) will continue to have ADHD as adults. Some follow-up studies have shown that 30% to 70% of children diagnosed as having ADHD continue to have either the full clinical picture or some residual symptoms as young adults.

Despite the clinical literature describing such a disorder in adults and the follow-up studies into adulthood that show that not all children with ADHD stop having the disorder after adolescence, the acceptance of ADHD in adults is not as clear as it should be. For example, in DSM-III-R there is no specific category for adults with ADHD.

At this time, neither the stimulants (Group I medications) nor the tricyclic antidepressants (Group II medications) have been approved by the Food and Drug Administration (FDA) for the treatment of ADHD in adults. Thus, if they are used, the adult must understand that there are clinical studies supporting the use of these medications with adults who have ADHD and that these medications are approved for use with adults with other disorders.

❖

Recognition

Few physicians who treat adults are familiar with ADHD. Similarly, few psychiatrists or other mental health professionals who work with adults think of the possibility of this disorder. Thus it is often missed. These adults may be recognized when the clinician establishes the diagnosis in a child or adolescent and a parent says, "That's me. I have the same problems." Or, one parent points to the other and says, "He [She] is just like [the child]." Some adults recognize the possible reason for their difficulties when they read a newspaper or magazine article about an individual who, as an adult, discovered that he or she had and still has this disability. Fortunately, more college mental health services have become aware of ADHD in adults and recognize the behaviors when they see them in a student.

The following case example involves a woman who was first diagnosed as having ADHD while in college:

❖ Case 1 ❖

Fran was diagnosed as having learning disabilities when she was in the third grade. Although she attended special classes all through high school, she had increasing difficulty doing her school work. Fran's teachers and her parents complained that she would not stay on task or complete her work. During her senior year of high school, she began psychotherapy. Her doctor placed her on an antidepressant, but she reported little benefit.

Fran went to a college that offered resource help and accommodations for her learning disabilities. Still, she found the work difficult. She couldn't concentrate when she studied in the dormitory and began to worry that she might not make it. On the advice of her former psychotherapist, she went to the college mental health service. The college psychologist who saw her suspected ADHD and referred her to me.

Fran gave a classic history of hyperactivity and distractibility throughout her life. She was fidgety and had been so "forever." Her friends, even her new ones in college, teased her about her constant need to move some part of her body. Any sound could distract her. She could recall examples from elementary school of listening to what was going on in the hall rather than in class. Fran cried as she described her impulsivity. She constantly hurt her friends' feelings by saying something before thinking, and her teachers often yelled at her for answering out of turn.

With Fran's permission, her mother was invited to a session. We asked her to bring all of Fran's old report cards and psychoeducational evaluations. The hyperactivity, distractibility, and impulsivity were described year after year, starting in kindergarten. The school and the parents assumed that these problems were part of her learning disability.

I started Fran on Ritalin. At a dose of 10 milligrams (mg) three times a day, she showed significant improvement: "It's a miracle. I feel so related. I can concentrate so much better, even in the dorm. I am getting my work done so much quicker and better. My friends have commented that I seem different. I pay attention when they are talking to me and I don't interrupt them when they are talking. . . . Why was I not given this medicine when I was a child?"

As with children or adolescents who have ADHD, it is important that the related problems be considered when establishing this diagnosis in an adult. Evidence of a learning disability should be looked for. This disability may have been recognized when the individual was in school, as with Fran, or may have been missed. Further, if the adult has emotional, social, or family problems, these difficulties might be secondary to or greatly impacted on by the ADHD and possible learning disabilities.

❖ **Diagnosis** ❖

As with children and adolescents, the diagnosis of ADHD for adults is made by establishing the presence of hyperactivity, distractibility, and/or impulsivity and by confirming that there is a chronic and pervasive history of these behaviors. The pervasiveness can be assessed by information provided by the individual. The chronic history might be confirmed by reviewing childhood and adolescent history, especially school history. Previous report cards and other school reports can be reviewed for evidence. If the parents are available, they might be asked. It is not uncommon to learn that such adults used to take medication as a child for "hyperactivity" or other related reasons. The hyperactivity, distractibility, and/or impulsivity might manifest itself differently in adults than it does in children or adolescents.

Hyperactivity

This behavior may have been present when the individual was younger. It often lessens or stops by adulthood. If it remains, it is more likely to be in the form of being fidgety. The individual, his or her family, friends, or people at work will describe a constant level of activity. Some adults report that they are always active. They have difficulty relaxing or sitting still at any time, even while at the movies or at a restaurant. They also may have difficulty falling asleep at night, and some report needing much less sleep than other people. Some find that the only way to relax and sleep is to exercise to the point of exhaustion. I have been impressed by the number of such adults who work out at a gym or run to the point of exhaustion each evening before coming home so that they can relax that night.

Distractibility

Distractibility is often the primary difficulty among adults with ADHD. The difficulty, just as with children or adolescents, is in handling unimportant visual or auditory stimuli in the environment, resulting in a short attention span. Some adults report what appears to be more of an internal distractibility. They may have trouble organizing their thoughts or may report difficulty doing tasks that require them to keep track of many units of information at a time. Sometimes, this problem becomes a major issue with success on a job or a promotion. Suddenly, with the new position, the individual has more need to be organized or to manage details of information relating to himself or herself and to others. The distractibility interferes with success.

Impulsivity

Adults with this problem, like children or adolescents, may speak or act before thinking. They might say things before they consider the impact of what they are saying on others. They might act impulsively, thus showing poor judgment. Some may appear to be more structured or compulsive than the average adult in an attempt to control their impulsivity.

❖   # Treatment   ❖

The treatment of ADHD in adults is the same as for children or adolescents. A multimodal approach including education, counseling, and the appropriate use of medication is needed.

Medication

As noted earlier, the FDA has not approved the use of Group I and Group II medications as a treatment of ADHD in adults. Thus the clinician must advise the individual before recommending treatment. The comments in this chapter on the use of medications are based on my own experiences. The approach to management of side effects, the initial medical evaluation, and the medical follow-up evaluations are considered to be the same as with children and adolescents and as discussed in earlier chapters. Each clinician must consider each patient and his or her needs in deciding how to approach treatment.

The effectiveness of the Group I medications do not appear to be related to body weight. I have had 200-pound men on 5 mg of Ritalin three times a day and 40-pound young children on 20 mg three times a day. The issues of dose, frequency of dose, and time coverage with stimulant medication must be addressed in the same way as was discussed for children and adolescents. As illustrated in the following case example, the use of the appropriate medication can be as successful in treating an adult with ADHD as it is in treating a child:

❖   Case 2   ❖

Michael, a 30-year-old attorney, came to see me after reading an article in the paper. He told me that from age nine to 16 he had been on medication because of overactivity and trouble concentrating. He remembered that two of his sisters took the same medicine. At my request, he contacted his parents, who contacted their family doctor. We learned that he had been on dextroamphetamine.

During college and law school Michael occasionally was able to get dextroamphetamine from his friends. When he took it, he studied better and more efficiently. Now, he was working for a law firm and having great difficulty staying on task and getting his work done. He said he was frustrated with his performance. He knew he could do the work, but he had great difficulty staying organized and keeping track of "billable hours."

I restarted Michael on dextroamphetamine. At a dose of 5 mg every four hours he reported a dramatic improvement. He was able to concentrate and stay on task. His thoughts were more organized, and he became effective and efficient at work. Even his supervisors noted the change.

If an adult responds positively to medication, the management of ADHD is the same as with children and adolescents. Many adults report that they function better with their family in the evening and on weekends if they are on the medication and, thus, request taking the medication seven days a week.

I have had a few adults with hyperactivity comment that they had become so used to "living with" this level of activity that they did not like the experience of being on medication. They felt too calm or sedated. Some adults have reported that they are so much more productive being hyperactive, working long hours, and needing little sleep. They now understand what the medication can do, yet they choose to stay off of the medication. I support this decision.

The Role of Therapy

If an adult is diagnosed as having ADHD and medication results in improvement, individual or group therapy might be recommended to help the individual understand himself or herself and the impact the ADHD has had on his or her life. It is not uncommon to find established emotional problems that need to be treated. Similarly, the ADHD behaviors may have had a significant impact on the individual's social interactions, resulting in poor social and interpersonal skills. These issues also must be addressed.

If learning disabilities are present, their impact must be addressed as well. Perhaps these disabilities were recognized and treated when the individual was a child, but no one has addressed the reality that these learning disabilities continue to impact on work and life demands. If they were never diagnosed, it will be necessary to explore how these disabilities have impacted on the individual's education and career. Major interventions may be needed to help identify the areas of disability, the impact these disabilities have had and continue to have on the individual, and what can be done at this time in the adult's life to help.

❖ <h2>Summary</h2>

Perhaps at least 25% of children with ADHD will continue to have this disability into their adulthood. The actual percentage is not yet known. It is important to consider this clinical possibility. The diagnosis and treatment are the same as they would be for a child or adolescent. The secondary emotional, social, and family problems may be significant and also must be addressed. If learning disabilities are found, they too must be clarified and addressed.

Legal Issues

Chapter 16

Legal Issues of Importance to Parents

Fortunately for your son or daughter, and for you, today there are laws that require school systems to provide services for students with disabilities. This was not always the case. Before 1975, about half of the handicapped children in the United States could not get an appropriate education. About one million were excluded from the public school system entirely. For the child with learning disabilities the situation was worse—about 90% were not even identified.

These laws, however, do not automatically assure that your child or adolescent will receive the educational programs he or she needs. This reality is even more true now because of the decrease in federal and state funding for education. You must know the laws and know your rights, and then you must work actively with the school while insisting on these rights. The school personnel care about the education of all students. You care especially about the education of your student.

What are these laws? What do they mean for your son or daughter? What must you know and do to assure the best help you can possibly get? What can you do if you are not pleased with your school's effort? In this chapter, I try to answer these questions.

❖ # Parent Power

The major force behind the legislation in place today was a consumer movement led by organizations of parents of handicapped children. Later, the handicapped people themselves joined in this effort. They focused on the lack of an appropriate public education and on the exclusion of children and adolescents from programs provided by the public education system.

In the 1960s, various groups of parents whose children had different handicaps, used publicity, mass mailings, public meetings, and other well-organized opinion-molding techniques to put pressure on state legislatures. They wanted laws making educational opportunities for the handicapped not simply available but mandatory. Most states responded with legislation, some more than others. A few states did nothing. Most of the more progressive state governments passed the laws but provided no enabling funds for facilities or trained professionals to carry out their intent. The focus of these pressure groups then shifted toward enactment of a federal law that could have an impact on all states.

In 1971, the Pennsylvania Association for Retarded Citizens filed a suit in Pennsylvania that directly involved the federal government in these issues for the first time. Citing constitutional guarantees of due process and equal protection under the law, they argued that the access of retarded children to public education should be equal to that afforded other children. The court agreed. A year later the Federal Court in the District of Columbia made a similar ruling involving not only people with mental retardation but those with a wide range of handicaps. This 1972 decision established two major precedents critical to future progress: 1) handicapped children have the right to a "suitable publicly supported education, regardless of the degree of the child's mental, physical, or emotional disability or impairment," and 2) concerning financing, "if sufficient funds are not available to finance all of the services and programs that are needed and desirable . . . the available funds must be expended equitably in such a manner that no child is entirely excluded from a publicly supported education." More than 40 such cases were won throughout the United States after these two landmark decisions.

These court actions also had a profound influence on federal legislation. The Rehabilitation Act of 1973, referred to as "The Civil Rights Act for the Handicapped," prohibits discrimination on the basis of physical or mental handicaps in every federally assisted program in the country. Public education, of course, accepts federal assistance. Section 504 of this law focuses on the rights of the individual people in these programs, and it has been the keystone of parents' demands and of numerous successful court actions. The most critical issues in this section are

1. As disabled job applicants or employees, handicapped people have the same rights and must be guaranteed the same benefits as nonhandicapped applicants and employees.
2. They are entitled to all of the medical services and medically related instruction that is available to the general public.
3. They are entitled to participate in vocational rehabilitation, day care, or any other social service program receiving federal assistance on an equal basis with the nonhandicapped.
4. They have the equal rights to go to college or to enroll in job-training or adult post–high-school basic education programs. Selection must be based on academic or other school records, and the disability cannot be a factor. (If a person has learning disabilities, the standard entrance testing procedures [such as the Scholastic Aptitude Test] can be modified, and admission standards can be based on potential as well as on past performance.)
5. State and local school districts must provide an appropriate elementary and secondary education for all handicapped students.

In 1990 this law was expanded to include all programs and not just federally funded programs. The required services and opportunities for the handicapped must be phased in over a time frame of several years.

This last part of Section 504 became the basis for Public Law 94-142, the "Education for All Handicapped Children Act," which was passed overwhelmingly by the House and Senate and enacted in November 1976. This landmark legislation capped a heroic effort begun by a few parents who joined with others to form organizations, these organizations then working together to lobby successfully for the needs of their children. The law is unique in several ways. There is no expiration date. It is regarded as permanent. It does more than just express a concern with handicapped children, it requires a specific commitment. The law sets forth as national policy the proposition that education must be extended to handicapped persons *as a fundamental right.*

Thanks to these parents, the right of persons with learning disabilities to a good education is now guaranteed by law. The rights of persons with ADHD are less clear. The challenge for today's parents is to insist on the transformation of this promise into reality.

Your need, as a parent, to educate yourself and to be appropriately assertive is more critical than ever. With federal, state, and county budget cuts, services to children who are handicapped have been significantly cut. Because of budget cuts and loss of personnel, some school systems lead parents to believe that their child is not entitled to services or that the minimal services offered are adequate. This crisis in services is compounded by another problem. The initial law, Public Law 94-142, provided services for parent education. There was an understood need to inform parents of their rights under the law. This knowledge helped parents enter the system and function within the system. The sons and daughters of these parents, however, have now graduated from high school. None of the parents with children currently in public schools benefited from this initial educational process. As I lecture around the country, I am distressed by the frequency with which I meet parents who do not know of their rights or how to fight for the services their son or daughter needs.

❖ Public Law 94-142: Education ❖ for All Handicapped Children Act

Because this law is so important to you, let me review first what the original law included and then explain the amendments enacted since. Also, let me suggest how you can work within this law to be an advocate for your child or adolescent.

The initial law listed 11 categories of handicapped children: mentally retarded, hard-of-hearing, deaf, deaf-blind, speech-impaired, visually handicapped, seriously emotionally disturbed, orthopedically impaired, other health-impaired, specific learning disabilities, and multi-handicapped. In a 1986 addition (discussed below), two groups were added: autism and traumatic brain injury.

Learning disabilities are listed and defined in Public Law 94-142. ADHD is not. Let me review learning disabilities first and then the status of ADHD.

The phrase "children with specific learning disabilities" is defined as applying to those children "who have a disorder in one or more of the basic psychological processes involved in understanding or in using language, spoken or written, which disorder may manifest itself in imperfect ability to listen, think, speak, read, write, spell, or do mathematical calculations. Such disorders include such conditions as perceptual handicaps, brain injury, minimal brain dysfunction, dyslexia, and developmental aphasia. Such term does not include children who have learning problems which are primarily the result of visual, hearing, or motor handicaps, or mental retardation, of emotional disturbance, or of environmental, cultural, or economic disadvantage."

There is no specific category in Public Law 94-142 for ADHD. In 1990–1991, a parent-based initiative attempted to have Congress add ADHD as a new category of disability. This effort did not fully succeed. The Department of Education was instructed to study ADHD and make recommendations back to Congress. At this time, a child or adolescent with ADHD can become eligible for services under this law under one of three existing categories. If the individual also has a learning disability, he or she can be eligible for services under the category *learning disabled.* If he or she has emotional problems, the category *seriously emotionally disturbed* can be used. If neither exists or is of major concern, an individual with ADHD can be eligible for services as *other health impaired.*

Specifically, the current law entitles children and adolescents with a handicapping condition to these rights:

1. A *free public education* is guaranteed to all between the ages of 3 and 21.
2. Each handicapped person is guaranteed an *individualized education program* (or *IEP*). This IEP must be in the form of a written

statement, jointly developed by the school officials, the child's teacher, the parents or guardians, and, if possible, by the child. It must include an analysis of the child's present achievement level, a list of both short-range and annual goals, an identification of the specific services that will be provided toward meeting these goals, and an indication of the extent to which the child will be able to participate in regular school programs. The IEP must also be clear about when these services will be provided and how long they will last, and it must provide a schedule for checking on the progress achieved under the plan and for making any revisions in it that may be needed.

3. Handicapped and nonhandicapped children must be *educated together* to the fullest extent that is appropriate. Children can be placed in special classes or separate schools only when the nature and severity of their handicap prevents satisfactory achievement in a regular education program.

4. Tests and other *evaluation materials* used in placing handicapped children must be prepared and administered in such a way as not to be racially or culturally discriminatory. They must also be presented in the child's native tongue.

5. An intensive and ongoing effort must be made to *locate* and *identify* children with handicaps, to evaluate their educational needs, and to determine whether these needs are being met.

6. In all efforts, *priority* must be given to those who are not receiving an education and to those severely handicapped people who are receiving an inadequate education.

7. In all decisions, a *prior consultation with the children's parents or guardians* must be held. No policies, programs, or procedures affecting the education of handicapped children may be adopted without a public notice.

8. These rights and guarantees apply to handicapped children *in private as well as public schools.* Any special education provided to any child shall be provided at no cost to the parents *if* state or local education agency officials placed the child in such schools or referred the child to them.

9. States and localities must develop comprehensive *personnel development programs,* including in-service training for regular as well

as special education teachers and support personnel.

10. In implementing the law, special effort shall be made to employ qualified handicapped persons.

11. All architectural barriers must be removed.

12. The state education agency has jurisdiction over all educational programs for handicapped children offered within a given state, including those administered by noneducational agencies.

13. An *advisory panel* must exist to advise the state's education agency of unmet needs. Membership must include handicapped people and parents or guardians of those people.

This law guarantees *procedural safeguards.* Parents or guardians have an opportunity to examine any records that bear on the identification of a child as being handicapped, on the defined nature and severity of their disability, and on the kind of educational setting in which they are placed. Schools must provide written notice before changing a child's placement. If a parent or guardian objects to a school's decision, there must be a process in place through which complaints can be registered. This process must include an opportunity for an impartial hearing that offers parents rights similar to those involved in a court case—the right to be advised by counsel (and by special education experts if they wish), to present evidence, to cross-examine witnesses, to compel the presence of any witnesses who do not appear voluntarily, to be provided a verbatim report of the proceedings, and to receive the decision and findings in written form.

The rights and safeguards of Public Law 94-142 are critical. Take the time to reread the above paragraph. Each school system is required to provide you a written guideline explaining your rights of appeal. If they have not done so, ask for it.

❖ Revisions to Public Law 94-142: ❖ Public Law 99-457

In September 1986, Congress passed Public Law 99-457. This law, titled the "Education of the Handicapped Act Amendments of 1986," includes provisions for handicapped children of all ages. The upper age was kept at 21 years. The original age of three years, however, was lowered to include "handicapped and 'at risk' children between the ages of birth and age six and their families."

There are two major components to this law. First, a new mandate for state education agencies to serve all three-, four-, and five-year-old handicapped children by 1990–1991 was created. All of the rights to an education in the original law for ages six to 21 are now required down to age three. As with the initial law, services for children aged three to six are not merely encouraged, but mandated. If a state does not comply it can lose many areas of federal funds. Second, Public Law 99-457 established the Handicapped Infants and Toddlers Program. This brand new federal program is designed to serve handicapped and at-risk children from birth to age three years and their families. Although this program is voluntary for states (that is, they may elect to not participate), those states choosing to participate or apply for funding under this law must meet the requirements of the law and assure that services are available for all eligible children. Public Law 99-457 stresses the importance of a coordinated and multiagency approach to the planning and dialogue that are necessary to implement the new early childhood initiatives. A wide variety of local providers, public and private, must work together to provide the services.

Finally, you should know about one last update. The 101st Congress approved a change in the name of Public Law 94-142 from "Education for All Handicapped Children" to "Individuals with Disabilities Education Act [IDEA]." The other change was to change the term *handicapped children* to *children with disabilities*.

❖ **Your Child or Adolescent** ❖
and Public Law 94-142

Each state has developed its own laws, rules, and regulations for carrying out the intentions of this federal law. Each must follow the federal guidelines. You will have to speak to your school officials, other parents, or other knowledgeable people to learn about the specifics as they apply in your state and community.

It is important for you to know the basic steps in the process used to help your son or daughter. The following list is a summary of these steps:

1. **Search:** Each school system should have a system for seeking out students who might have a disability.
2. **Find:** Once a student with a potential problem is identified, there should be a system for collecting information and designing an evaluation process.
3. **Evaluation:** A comprehensive and multidisciplinary evaluation should be done.
4. **Conference:** Parents or guardians should meet with the school personnel and evaluation professionals to review the evaluation conclusions, any labels or diagnoses established, and any proposed placement and IEP, the details of which should be presented in writing.
5. **Parents' decision process:** Parents or guardians, with consultation from educational or other professionals and lawyers when needed, decide to accept, request clarification, request changes, or reject the proposed placement and IEP.
6. **Appeals process:** If parents reject the label or diagnosis, placement recommendation, or IEP, there should be an appeals process that starts with the local school system and can go to the county or state level.
7. **Follow-up:** Progress reports should be provided to the family. As the end of the school year approaches, a reassessment is done (with many school systems, a full, formal reevaluation is done only every three years). There should be a conference to plan the next year. Steps 5 and 6 are repeated before implementing the next year's plans.

This federal law requires every school system within each state to meet the requirements of the law. School systems can only get away with not meeting the requirements of the law if parents do not know their rights. Because this is so important, let me go into more detail about the steps in the process.

Search

If someone from your school system suggests that your son or daughter has a problem and wants to do some tests, be positive and agree to the testing. If the tests reveal a problem, you can get help. If the tests reveal that there is nothing wrong, that should relieve both you and the school.

If you are concerned about your child's academic progress and suspect a problem but the school has said nothing about it, speak to the classroom teacher. Share your observations and concerns. If the teacher agrees with you, he or she can initiate the process through the principal. If you cannot get the classroom teacher to start this process, meet with the principal. (It is better not to go directly to the principal first because this may antagonize the teacher.) When there are two parents, it is always better for both to be present at such meetings. Explain your concerns again, and ask the principal to start the evaluation process. If the principal does not agree and/or refuses to request such an evaluation, contact the head of the special education (or special services) team assigned to your school and request the evaluation. You have the right to go above the principal's head once you have met with him or her. In many school systems, if a parent requests an evaluation in writing to the principal, the principal *must* forward the request to the evaluation team within 30 working days.

When you reach the person at the special education office, get his or her name. Explain your concerns and make it clear that you have already spoken to the teacher and the principal. Ask if this person or someone else could observe your child and then meet with the teacher and you.

These efforts should result in an evaluation or a very substantial reason why one is not required. If you are still not successful, several other strategies may work. You can send a letter to your superintendent of schools, explaining why you are concerned, what you have done, and what you believe you are entitled to under Federal Law 94-142 (quote from the material in this book). Always send a copy of your letter to the person in the special education office, the principal, and the teacher. Request a meeting. At best, you will have the meeting. At the very least, pressure will be building on the evaluation team to do something.

Hopefully, you will get the evaluation. You also can have the evaluation done privately. If significant results are found, they can be presented to the principal and the special education staff.

Find

Once the school agrees to the need for an evaluation, make yourself as informed as possible about what the evaluation is and what is being assessed. Find out what is planned, make sure that the plans cover the areas discussed in the chapter on the evaluation process. Be sure that someone prepares your son or daughter for each step.

Conference

School personnel and special educators will meet with you. If possible, both parents or guardians should be present. You may also bring your own professional consultant to review the results and recommendations and to advise you. If necessary, you could bring your lawyer.

Angry, defensive, or demanding behavior won't get you anyplace. Assume that everyone at the conference has the best interest of your son or daughter at heart. In reality, this is true for most school conferences. Listen, ask questions, and reflect. Even if you agree completely with everything that is advised, ask for time to think about and read the recommendations in detail. On one hand, anger or defensiveness polarizes the sides. On the other, too quick an agreement may prevent you from asking questions that occur to you after you read the reports and reflect on them.

Do your homework before the conference. Talk with other parents who have been in the same situation and, if possible, learn something about what programs are likely to be suggested.

During the conference, ask questions. If someone says that your child has learning disabilities, ask for specifics. You know what learning disabilities are. Impress them with your awareness and their need to be precise. Don't let the evaluator(s) overwhelm you with professional words. Ask for definitions and clarification in a calm, concerned way. Let them know that although what they say is important, this is *your* child or adolescent about whom you care very much.

Remember, for the school professionals, the question at this conference is not whether your son or daughter has a learning disability; the question is whether he or she is eligible for services. Each school system has a definition of eligibility based on a discrepancy formula (that is, how far behind the child or adolescent has to be in certain areas to qualify for services). It has been my experience that when the budget is adequate the amount of discrepancy between ability and performance required to be eligible for services is small and when the budget is tight the formula is changed to require a greater discrepancy.

If you don't agree with the findings, don't challenge them just now. Tell the evaluation team that you would like a copy of the test results to show to another professional for a second opinion. You wouldn't consent to your child having open heart surgery or even to being sent to the hospital without a second opinion. Committing your child to at least one year of a special education program or to another year in a regular program without the appropriate help has just as great an impact on his or her life.

You will have to agree to the diagnosis, or label (that is, to the name the school gives to the problems they say your son or daughter has). You also will have to agree to the placement recommendations and IEP proposed. Ask for clarifications and definitions. Read the documents carefully and be sure you understand.

Keep in mind the difference between an emotional problem that *causes* academic difficulties and one that *results* in an academic difficulty. If your son's or daughter's behavior problems are due to the frustrations and failures experienced because of ADHD plus possibly learning disabilities, don't agree to having him or her labeled "emotionally disturbed." If the school personnel insist that your son or daughter has learning disabilities and an emotional disorder, they are probably correct. In making your decision, consider this possibility. If your child is coded as "learning disabled" first and as "emotionally disturbed" second, the placement will be in a program for students with learning disabilities with supportive psychological help. If he or she is coded as "emotionally disturbed" first and as "learning disabled" second, the placement will be in a program for students with emotional disorders with supportive special education help for the learning disabilities. Which do you believe would be best for your child? The primary label is critical. Fight for the correct one.

Your school system is responsible for placing your child in an appropriate program within their system. Only if this is not possible will they consider an out-of-system or private placement. You may prefer that your child go into a particular private program that you know about. The school does not have to concur, however, if an appropriate placement is available within their own system. You might argue that the private placement is better, and this might be true. But even if it is true, the law states only that each child must receive an *appropriate* education, not necessarily the *best* education possible.

The necessary services can be provided at several levels of intensity. You want to find the *least restrictive program* that still provides the *most effective educational support* for your child. Remember that this does not always mean being in a program that resembles a regular class program. The least restrictive environment for some children might be the most restrictive environment available. A child may need the security and support of a small, separate, self-contained classroom to feel safe enough to relax and become available for learning.

Ask for the details on any placement. Where is it? Will your child have to be transported out of the neighborhood? Ask about the qualifications of the teacher, the size of the class, and the age distribution of the students. Ask about the other children in the class, including their diagnoses and levels of intellectual functioning. Ask if you can visit the program. Even if it is spring and you will see a different group of students, you will get a feel for the teacher and program. Try to speak to several parents of the children currently in the program. If the teacher has not been selected or the class makeup established yet, ask for a written statement of the qualifications that this teacher must have and the probable makeup of the class.

What about the IEP? This is the written plan identifying the instruction designed especially for your son or daughter and listing reasonable expectations for his or her achievement. There should be a specific system for monitoring progress. At a minimum, each IEP must cover the following points:

1. A statement of your child's levels of educational performance.
2. A statement of yearly goals or achievements expected for each area of identified weakness by the end of the school year.
3. Short-term objectives stated in instructional terms, which are the steps leading to the mastery of these yearly goals.
4. A statement of the specific special education and support services to be provided to the child.

5. A statement of the extent to which a child will be able to participate in regular education programs and justification for any special placement recommended.
6. Projected dates for initiation of services and the anticipated duration of the services.
7. A statement of the criteria and evaluation procedures to be used in determining, on at least an annual basis, whether short-term objectives are being achieved.

In addition to an appropriate placement and IEP, your child may need other services. These are called *related services,* and they are to be provided at no expense to the family. The formal definition of related services includes "transportation and such developmental, corrective, and other supportive services (including speech pathology and audiology, psychological services, physical and occupational therapy, recreation, and medical counseling services, except that such medical services shall be for diagnostic and evaluation purposes only) as may be required to assist a handicapped child to benefit from special education, and includes the early identification and assessment of handicapping conditions in children." These services are usually provided by the school system and built into the school program.

Related services are expensive. Your school personnel might make many suggestions about getting the child or adolescent into psychotherapy but never formally recommend it verbally or in writing. They know that if they recommend a service, thus identifying it as a related service, the school system must pay for the service.

Parents' Decision Process

After the conference, you are entitled to a full transcript of the meeting. You can also get copies of all tests that were done. The placement and the IEP recommendations must also be provided in writing.

Read all of the documents. If necessary, ask for clarification or more details. If you see something in writing that was not mentioned at the meeting, ask for an explanation. If you need help, seek consultation and advice from other parents or from professionals.

If you are comfortable with the school's plan for your child or adolescent, you may agree to it and sign the necessary documents. If you do not agree and cannot get the school personnel to modify their proposals, inform them that you wish to appeal. Ask that they review with you their appeal process. Remember that you are entitled by law to due process of appeal.

Appeals Process

The appeals process differs with each state and local school system. Your school system is suppose to have the step-by-step process in writing for you. If you feel that you need legal guidance, try to find a lawyer who works in the area of special education law. Other parents may be of help in finding the right person. The final step in this appeals process is usually a meeting between you and your school system before a "hearing officer" who is not part of the school system. The hearing officer's decision is binding. It is usually best to have legal help if you get to this level.

The appeals process may go quickly or may take months. Meanwhile your son or daughter must attend school. You might decide to accept a placement and IEP under protest, allowing an educational program to begin while the appeals process proceeds.

Follow-up

If your son or daughter is in a special education program, the professionals involved should meet with you every 60 to 90 school days to review your child's progress. At the end of each school year, plans should be presented for the next school year.

❖ Implementation ❖

The best designed plans of April and May can fall apart in September. Be observant when school opens. Be sure the placement, the teacher, the related services, the makeup of the class, and the implementation steps for the IEP are correct and in operation. Be concerned, ask questions, but try not to be a nuisance. If you believe that some departure from the plan agreed on has been made, ask about it.

Be sure that the regular classroom teachers with whom your child has contact are aware of any special needs or programs. Be certain that they are familiar with the evaluation and the IEP and that they are in regular contact with the special education professionals.

As discussed earlier, programs begun in September may get changed or diluted as the year progresses and the number of students in need of service increases. Ask your son or daughter to keep you informed or check this for yourself. Does each person see your son or daughter the amount of time noted in the IEP? Are more children being added to the program, thus diluting the time your child or adolescent receives services? Know your child's IEP and insist that he or she gets what it promises. Remember that no changes can be made without a written notification and your concurrence.

❖ Other Thoughts ❖

Your son or daughter must be kept informed. How much you share, what you explain, and how you explain it will depend on the child's age. If you need help, ask the professionals involved to meet with you and your child or adolescent. If you think it would be helpful, make it a family session.

I touched earlier on how to handle any resistance by your son or daughter to accepting help. Let me mention one other problem—stigma. Other children can be cruel, sometimes on purpose, sometimes they just say all the wrong things. The child or adolescent may be teased about taking medication. The special programs may be called "retard" or "mental" classes, and the children in them may be called "retards" or "speds" (for *special education*). It all hurts. Speak to the teachers. Ask that they talk to the offending students. Perhaps the teachers could discuss the theme of being different with the whole class. Alert the teacher if his or her insensitivity contributes to the teasing. If necessary, speak to the parents of an offending child in as positive a way as you can. (Here, as elsewhere, hostility will not get you very far.)

Support your child and empathize with his or her feelings. Don't be afraid to show your own emotions and don't be afraid to have a good cry together. You would do anything in the world to spare your child these problems, but they exist. Make sure your child knows that you care too much to ignore what is going on and that you will do everything possible to support and help. Keep at it until the teasing is minimized or stopped.

Work closely with your school personnel, and make them work closely with you. As a team, the school and the family can do the best job of helping your son or daughter reach his or her maximum growth and potential.

❖ ADHD and the Individuals ❖ With Disabilities Education Act

At the time this book was being prepared, ADHD was not included as a specific type of disability in the federal law. As mentioned earlier, a parent group did try to have ADHD listed as a specific disability; however, Congress did not agree. Instead, the U.S. Department of Education has been asked to study this question and to report back to Congress.

Of importance is a U.S. Department of Education memorandum issued in September 1991 by the Assistant Secretary, Office of Special Education and Rehabilitative Services; the Assistant Secretary, Office for Civil Rights; and the Assistant Secretary, Office of Elementary and Secondary Education. The intent was to clarify the policy for addressing the needs of children with "attention deficit disorders" (ADD) within general and/or special education. This memorandum clarifies that all state and local educational agencies must provide special education and related services to eligible children with "ADD."

The U.S. Department of Education did not support a new category for ADHD. Instead, this memorandum clarified that a student with "ADD" can become eligible for services by being identified under the "other health impaired" category. If the student also has a learning disability, he or she can become eligible for services by being identified under the "specific learning disability" category. Similarly, he or she can become eligible for services by being identified under the "seriously emotionally disturbed" category.

This memorandum also addressed the guidelines under Section 504 of the Rehabilitation Act of 1973. This is the section that provides a free appropriate public education to each qualified handicapped child. If parents believe that their child has "ADD," the school must evaluate the child to determine whether he or she is handicapped. If the evaluation reveals the child is handicapped, the guidelines described earlier must be followed.

In this memorandum, school systems are instructed to take the necessary steps to promote coordination between special and regular education programs. Steps are also mentioned to train regular education teachers and other personnel to develop their awareness about "ADD" and its manifestations, as well as the adaptations that can be implemented in regular education programs.

Conclusions

Chapter 17

Conclusions

A ttention-deficit hyperactivity disorder (ADHD) is a life disability. It impacts on all aspects of life. For many individuals, ADHD is also a lifetime disability. Depending on the study used, between 30% and 70% of children with this disorder will continue to have symptoms of ADHD as an adult. Like any other developmental disorder, especially a developmental disorder that may be a chronic disorder, the consequences of not recognizing, diagnosing, and fully treating ADHD can be extensive. Each stage of psychosocial development can be affected, as can academic success, self-esteem, and peer interactions. Significant emotional, social, and family problems can become as great a disability for the adult as is the primary disability of ADHD. The secondary academic underachievement might impact on the work career and on work success.

Thus the recognition, diagnosis, and treatment of ADHD in children, adolescents, and adults are critical. Missing the diagnosis or not treating the disorder properly can result in a lifetime of disability. It is important for parents to know of this disorder and to be alert to the possibility that their daughter or son might have it. It is critical that health and mental health professionals know of this disorder and be alert to its possible presence. Of equal importance is the need to look for the associated disorders, especially learning disabilities.

If ADHD has caused secondary emotional, social, and family problems, they too must be addressed. It is important to remember that the treatment of these difficulties will not be successful unless the primary disorder, ADHD, is identified and treated.

The first step in treatment is to do a full evaluation and to find each area of difficulty. The treatment plan must address each problem area.

The treatment of choice for ADHD is multimodal. Parent and individual education and counseling usually is first. Specific behavioral management approaches might be needed. The use of appropriate medications is essential. Further individual, behavioral, group, and/or family therapy might be needed. Throughout each effort, it is necessary to work closely with the school.

Today, many educational, health, and mental health professionals are not familiar with ADHD. Thus it is essential that you, as parents, become fully educated. You may have to take the initiative to educate the professional you are working with.

It is hoped that this book will be useful to you in understanding the recognition, diagnosis, and treatment of children, adolescents, and adults with ADHD and that this book will help you as you work closely with education, health, and mental health professionals.

You must be that special parent who is informed and assertive so that you can help your son or daughter with ADHD and help your family. I hope this book helps you be that special parent.

Best of success in helping your child or adolescent grow into a happy, healthy, productive adult.

Suggested Readings

T here are many excellent books available on attention-deficit hyperactivity disorder (ADHD). I list many of them below. Each has an extensive reference section for those parents who want to read more on a particular area. One of the books noted is an extensive review of the literature and might be the best first book for those who need more. Because many books are almost out of date by the time they are published, it would be best for a reader who wants or needs an extensive literature review on a specific topic covered in this book to do a computer search and obtain a printout of the most current information.

This list presents the books I believe to be most helpful and a description of their contents.

- *Your Hyperactive Child: A Parents' Guide to Coping with Attention Deficit Disorder,* by Barbara Ingersoll, Ph.D. (Doubleday, New York, 1988)

This is book for parents. The focus is on recognition, diagnosis, and treatment. Dr. Ingersoll discusses specific approaches and suggestions for parents to help their child.

■ *The Hyperactive Child, Adolescent, and Adult: Attention Deficit Disorder Through the Lifespan,* by Paul H. Wender, M.D. (Oxford Press, New York, 1987)

This book for parents and professionals reviews the diagnosis and models of treatment for ADHD with children, adolescents, and adults. The section on adults is especially helpful.

■ *Hyperactive Children Grown Up,* by Gabrielle Weiss, M.D., and Lily Trokenberg Hechtman, M.D. (Guilford Press, New York, 1986)

This book is a review of research started in 1961. Drs. Weiss and Trokenberg Hechtman discuss their research as well as that of others, focusing on known information and controversial information. By using their long-term follow-up data, they try to identify patterns. Using these patterns they suggest predictors that might suggest outcome. Of particular interest is a chapter on the adults' views of their life experiences and their treatment as children and adolescents. A comprehensive bibliography follows each chapter.

■ *Learning Disabilities: Proceedings of the National Conference,* edited by James F. Kavanagh, Ph.D., and Tom J. Truss, Jr., Ph.D. (York Press, Parkton, Maryland, 1988)

In 1986–1987 an Interagency Committee was established by Congress to review and assess the federal activities relating to learning disabilities. As part of this initiative, several experts·in specific topic areas were asked to review the literature on their topic. This book consists of each of these literature reviews. Several papers provide an extensive review of the literature on Learning Disabilities (by Doris J. Johnson, Ph.D.) and Language Disabilities (by Paula Tallal, Ph.D.). The paper on Hyperactivity/Attention Deficits by Sally E. Shaywitz, M.D., and Bennett E. Shaywitz, M.D., is an outstanding review of the research literature on this topic. There is an extensive bibliography following each section.

■ *The Misunderstood Child: A Guide for Parents of Children With Learning Disabilities,* Second Edition, by Larry B. Silver, M.D. (TAB/McGraw-Hill, New York, 1992)

This book is written for parents. It reviews the disorders of learning disabilities and ADHD. The history of each disorder is reviewed, as well as how the problems are recognized and diagnosed. The major focus is on parent education, teaching parents to understand their son or daughter and to build on strengths rather than magnify weaknesses in helping him or her grow psychologically and socially. Parents are taught how to be advocates, fighting to get appropriate and necessary evaluations and treatments. They become informed consumers, knowing what is known about each disorder.

■ *ADHD: Attention Deficit-Hyperactivity Disorder and Learning Disabilities: Booklet for Parents,* by Larry B. Silver (1991)

■ *ADHD: Attention Deficit-Hyperactivity Disorder and Learning Disabilities: Booklet for the Classroom Teacher,* by Larry B. Silver (1991)

■ *ADHD: Attention Deficit-Hyperactivity Disorder and Learning Disabilities: Booklet for Physicians,* by Larry B. Silver (1991)

Each of these booklets offers a brief review of ADHD and learning disabilities for the audience noted in the title. Each relates to the other. For example, the booklet for physicians notes the need to obtain information from the teacher. The booklet for the teacher comments that the child's physician may ask for certain information, then explains what information to provide. Each is available to clinicians at no charge (and in quantity) from CIBA-Geigy Pharmaceuticals, 555 Morris Avenue, Summit, New Jersey 08901

■ *Attention Deficit Hyperactivity Disorder: A Handbook for Diagnosis and Treatment,* by Russell A. Barkley, Ph.D. (Guilford Press, New York, 1990)

Dr. Barkley has written an excellent and extensive review of the current literature on this disorder. In addition, he discusses in detail his research and concepts of ADHD. Chapters cover all topic areas with a detailed discussion of research. There is a full bibliography at the end of each chapter.

■ *Managing Attention Disorders in Children: A Guide for Practitioners,* by Sam Goldstein, Ph.D., and Michael Goldstein, M.D. (John Wiley & Sons, New York, 1990)

This book focuses on assessment and treatment. The chapters on management, social skill training, and working with teachers are especially helpful.

■ *Attention-Deficit Hyperactivity Disorder: A Clinical Guide to Diagnosis and Treatment,* by Larry B. Silver, M.D. (American Psychiatric Press, Washington, DC, 1991)

This book is written for physicians and for other health and mental health professionals. It follows the same topic areas outlined in this book. It is intended to help these professionals better understand ADHD and the roles they must play in helping the child, adolescent, and family. (You might want to get this book to give to your family physician or to other clinicians.)

■ *Diagnostic and Statistical Manual of Mental Disorders,* Third Edition, Revised (American Psychiatric Association, Washington, DC, 1987)

This is the current diagnostic manual referred to throughout this book. It should be available in libraries or can be ordered from the American Psychiatric Association, 1400 K Street, N.W., Washington, DC 20005.

Appendix B

Resources for Professionals and for Families

There are many parent and professional organizations that are helpful to clinicians who see individuals with attention-deficit hyperactivity disorder (ADHD), families of children and adolescents with ADHD, and adults with ADHD. Many of these organizations have state, county, and local groups.

Local groups are most helpful. Because such groups often change in location or start new, I list here only the national offices for each. The clinician or family can contact this national office for the location of the closest group or chapter.

❖ Parent Organizations ❖

Attention Deficit Disorder Association (ADDA)
8091 South Ireland Way
Aurora, Colorado 80016
(800) 487-2282

A national alliance of ADHD support groups that provides referrals and information to parents and parent support groups.

Children With Attention Deficit Disorders (Chadd)
Suite 185
1859 North Pine Island Road
Plantation, Florida 33322
(305) 857-3700

A national alliance of parent organizations that provides information
and support to parents of children with ADHD.

Learning Disabilities Association of America (LDA)
4156 Library Road
Pittsburgh, Pennsylvania 15234
(412) 341-1515

A national organization with state, county, and local chapters for parents of children and adolescents with learning disabilities and adults
with learning disabilities. Provides information on the disorder and on
available services.

**National Information Center for Handicapped Children
and Youth**
P.O. Box 1492
Washington, DC 20013

An information clearinghouse that provides newsletters, fact sheets,
issue briefs, brochures, booklets, and a listing of state and local organizations relating to different handicapping conditions.

Tourette Syndrome Association
42-40 Bell Boulevard
Bayside, New York 11361

An information and support organization that both works with parents
and professionals and encourages and supports research.

❖ **Professional Organizations** ❖

American Academy of Child and Adolescent Psychiatry
3615 Wisconsin Avenue, N.W.
Washington, DC 20016
(202) 966-7300

American Academy of Pediatrics
P.O. Box 927
141 Northwest Point Boulevard
Elk Grove Village, Illinois 60009
(708) 981-7935

American Occupational Therapy Association
1383 Piccard Drive
Rockville, Maryland 20850
(301) 948-9626

American Psychiatric Association
1400 K Street, N.W.
Washington, DC 20005
(202) 682-6000

American Psychological Association
750 1st Street, NE
Washington, DC 20002
(202) 336-5500

American Speech, Language, and Hearing Association
10801 Rockville Pike
Rockville, Maryland 20852
(301) 897-5700

Council for Exceptional Children
1920 Association Drive
Reston, Virginia 22091
(703) 620-3660

Includes an Education Resources Information Center (ERIC) on handicapped and gifted children that provides information and a clearinghouse.

National Association of Social Workers
7981 Eastern Avenue
Silver Spring, Maryland 20901
(301) 565-0333

Orton Dyslexia Society
724 York Road
Baltimore, Maryland 21204
(301) 296-0232

Sensory Integration International
1402 Cravens Avenue
Torrance, California 90501

❖ **Other Organizations** ❖

National Center for Learning Disabilities
99 Park Avenue
New York, New York 10016
(212) 687-7211

This organization provides publications and other public awareness and public education initiatives for parents, professionals, and the public.

Self Help Clearing House
St. Claire's Riverside Medical Center
Pocono Road
Denville, New Jersey 07834
(201) 625-9565

Resource center that provides local and national referral services. Computerized database of support groups and referral agencies nationwide is available.

Index

Page numbers printed in **boldface** *refer to tables or figures.*

Index

Index

Education for All Handicapped
  Children Act. *See* Public Law
  94-142
Education of the Handicapped Act
  Amendments of 1986, 225–226
Elimination diets. *See* Diet and
  ADHD
Embarrassment, 100–101
Emotional lability, 181, 188
Emotional problems, 26–28, 85–86
  in adults with ADHD, 214
  anxiety, 26
  concomitant with ADHD, 7
  depression, 26–27
  differences from ADHD, 19–20
  treatment planning for, 127
Environmental factors, 119
Epilepsy, 8–9, 119
Equal, 203

Family
  evaluation of, 131
  problems in, 7
  studies of, 116
  treatment planning for, 127
Family
  education of, 133–136
Family reactions, 91–112
  acceptance of child's differences,
    92
  case example of, 102–112
    current progress note, 111–112
    delivery and first year, 103–105
    pregnancy, 103
    year three, 107–110
    years one and two, 105–106
    years three through twelve,
      110–111
  parental
    normal, 92–96

  pathological, 96–98
  of siblings, 98–102
Family therapy, 131, 145, 148–149
Feingold, Benjamin, 199–203
Fetal development, 118–119
Fever, 190–191
Fidgetiness. *See* Hyperactivity
Fighting, 85
  among siblings, 100
Figure-ground problem
  auditory, 24, 45
  visual, 44–45
Fire-setting, 18
Food additives and preservatives,
    200. *See also* Diet and ADHD
Food allergies, 204–205
Frustration, 85

Genetic factors, 116
Girls with ADHD, 10, 115–116
Group therapy, 131
  for adults with ADHD, 214
Guilt
  of parents, 94–96, 104
    chronic, 97–98
  of siblings, 101

Head injury, 119
Headache, 85, 187
Height growth impairment, 188–189
Historical descriptions, 3–5
Hitting, 85
*How Psychiatry Is Making Drug
  Addicts out of America's
  Children*, 138
Hyperactivity, 5–6, 15–16, 22–24,
    106. *See also* Behavioral
    problems
  in adults, 212
  allergies and, 204–205